A Note From Rick Renner

I am on a personal quest to see a "revival of the Bible" so people can establish their lives on a firm foundation that will stand strong and endure the test when the end-time storm winds begin to intensify.

In order to experience a revival of the Bible in your personal life, it is important to take time each day to read, receive, and apply its truths to your life. James tells us that if we will continue in the perfect law of liberty — refusing to be forgetful hearers but determined to be doers — we will be blessed in our ways. As you watch or listen to the programs in this series and work through this corresponding study guide, I trust that you will search the Scriptures and allow the Holy Spirit to help you hear something new from God's Word that applies specifically to your life. I encourage you to be a doer of the Word that He reveals to you. Whatever the cost, I assure you — it will be worth it.

> Thy words were found, and I did eat them;
> and thy word was unto me the joy and rejoicing of mine heart:
> for I am called by thy name, O Lord God of hosts.
> — Jeremiah 15:16

Your brother and friend in Jesus Christ,

Rick Renner

Unless otherwise indicated, all scripture quotations are taken from the *King James Version* of the Bible.

Scripture quotations marked (*AMPC*) are taken from the *Amplified® Bible*. Copyright © 1954, 1958, 1962, 1964, 1965, 1987 by The Lockman Foundation. Used by permission. **www.Lockman.org**.

Scripture quotations marked (*NIV*) are taken from *Holy Bible, New International Version®, NIV®* Copyright ©1973, 1978, 1984, 2011 by Biblica, Inc.® Used by permission. All rights reserved worldwide.

Scripture quotations marked (*MSG*) are taken from *The Message*, copyright © 1993, 2002, 2018 by Eugene H. Peterson. Used by permission of NavPress. All rights reserved. Represented by Tyndale House Publishers, Inc.

Scripture quotations marked (*NKJV*) are taken from the *New King James Version®*. Copyright © 1982 by Thomas Nelson. Used by permission. All rights reserved.

Scripture quotations marked (*NLT*) are taken from the Holy Bible, *New Living Translation*, copyright © 1996, 2004, 2015 by Tyndale House Foundation. Used by permission of Tyndale House Publishers, Inc., Carol Stream, Illinois 60188. All rights reserved.

The Coming of the Antichrist

Copyright © 2020 by Rick Renner
8316 E. 73rd St.
Tulsa, Oklahoma 74133

Published by Rick Renner Ministries
www.renner.org

ISBN 13: 978-1-68031-746-6

eBook ISBN 13: 978-1-68031-747-3

All rights reserved. No portion of this book may be reproduced or transmitted in any form or by any means — electronic, mechanical, photocopy, recording, scanning, or other — except for brief quotations in critical reviews or articles, without the prior written permission of the Publisher.

How To Use This Study Guide

This ten-lesson study guide corresponds to *"The Coming of the Antichrist" With Rick Renner* (**Renner TV**). Each lesson in this study guide covers a topic that is addressed during the program series, with questions and references supplied to draw you deeper into your own private study of the Scriptures on this subject.

To derive the most benefit from this study guide, consider the following:

First, watch or listen to the program prior to working through the corresponding lesson in this guide. (Programs can also be viewed at **renner.org** by clicking on the Media/Archives links.)

Second, take the time to look up the scriptures included in each lesson. Prayerfully consider their application to your own life.

Third, use a journal or notebook to make note of your answers to each lesson's Study Questions and Practical Application challenges.

Fourth, invest specific time in prayer and in the Word of God to consult with the Holy Spirit. Write down the scriptures or insights He reveals to you.

Finally, take action! Whatever the Lord tells you to do according to His Word, do it.

For added insights on this subject, it is recommended that you obtain Rick Renner's book *Last Days Survival Guide: A Scriptural Handbook To Prepare You for These Perilous Times*. You may also select from Rick's other available resources by placing your order at **renner.org** or by calling 1-800-742-5593.

LESSON 1

TOPIC

The Rapture of the Church

SCRIPTURES

1. **1 Thessalonians 4:15-17** — For this we say unto you by the word of the Lord, that we which are alive and remain unto the coming of the Lord shall not prevent them which are asleep. For the Lord himself shall descend from heaven with a shout, with the voice of the archangel, and with the trump of God: and the dead in Christ shall rise first. Then we which are alive and remain shall be caught up together with them in the clouds, to meet the Lord in the air: and so shall we ever be with the Lord.
2. **Luke 18:8** — ...When the Son of man cometh, shall he find faith on the earth?

GREEK WORDS

1. "are alive" — **οἱ ζῶντες** (*hoi zontes*): the living ones; the vibrant ones; not lifeless and dead
2. "remain" — **οἱ περιλειπόμενοι** (*hoi perileipomenoi*): the remaining ones; surviving ones; those who are left, indicating possibly "not many"; coincides with 2 Thessalonians 2:3
3. "(to) find" — **εὑρίσκω** (*heurisko*): to find or discover; pictures a discovery made as a result of careful observance; a moment when one makes a conclusive discovery; usually points to a discovery made due to intense investigation, scientific study, or scholarly research
4. "faith" — **τὴν πίστιν** (*ten pistin*): in context, with a definite article; "the faith"
5. "unto" — **εἰς** (*eis*): unto; right unto
6. "coming" — **παρουσία** (*parousia*): a technical expression for the royal visit of a king or emperor; the arrival of one who alone can deal with a situation
7. "them which are asleep" — **τοὺς κοιμηθέντας** (*tous koimethentas*): from **κοιμάω** (*koimao*); to sleep; to sleep deeply; the sleep of death; where we get the words "coma" and "catacomb"

8. "descend" — **καταβαίνω** (*katabaino*): compound of **κατά** (*kata*) and **βαίνω** (*baino*); the word **κατά** (*kata*) means down, and **βαίνω** (*baino*) means to step; to come down; to move downward from a higher place to a lower place; to descend; pictures downward movement with a dominating force
9. "from heaven" — **ἀπ' οὐρανοῦ** (*ap' ouranou*): directly from the heaven
10. "shout" — **κέλευσμα** (*keleusma*): a direct order or command; used to arouse horses, charioteers, hounds, hunters, rowers, masters of ships, etc.; a signal given like a trumpet call to muster troops to action
11. "voice" — **φωνή** (*phone*): voice; sound; noise; to whirl; depicts the sound of wind, wings, water; may depict the sound of a massive multitude; an overwhelming sound
12. "trump of God" — **σάλπιγγι Θεοῦ** (*salpingi Theou*): the root word **σάλπιγξ** (*salpingx*) depicts a war trumpet that calls to war; a war trumpet that announces battle and, predictively, ultimate victory and the vanquishing of enemies at the very outset of a military campaign; used in the Old Testament for when God summons His people to war
13. "the dead in Christ" — **οἱ νεκροὶ ἐν Χριστῷ** (*hoi nekroi en Christos*): from root word **νεκρός** (*nekros*), a lifeless corpse
14. "shall rise" — **ἀναστήσονται** (*anastesontai*): from **ἀνίστημι** (*anistemi*), to stand again; to rise; to be resurrected; used to depict a rising of kings and rulers
15. "first — **πρῶτον** (*proton*): first in order; in first place; to begin with
16. "then" — **ἔπειτα** (*epeita*): upon that moment; exactly at that moment; exactly then
17. "we which are alive" — **οἱ ζῶντες** (*hoi zontes*): the living ones; to be alive, not lifeless and dead
18. "remain" — **οἱ περιλειπόμενοι** (*hoi perileipomenoi*): remaining ones; surviving ones; those who are left, indicating possibly not many
19. "caught up together" — **ἁρπαγησόμεθα** (*harpagesometha*): a form of **ἁρπάζω** (*harpadzo*); to catch, seize, take away; to snatch suddenly; to snatch just in time
20. "meet" — **ἀπάντησις** (*apantesis*): to the meeting; to the reception; to the encounter; a technical word used for the reception of a newly arrived official or royalty
21. "air" — **ἀέρα** (*aera*): air; the lower regions of the heavens; the lower atmosphere

22. "ever be" — πάντοτε (*pantote*): at all times; all the time; always; continually; perpetually

SYNOPSIS

The ten lessons in this study on *The Coming of the Antichrist* will focus on the following topics:

- The Rapture of the Church
- In the Twinkling of an Eye
- Inaccurate Prophecy Teachers
- A Worldwide Mutiny Against God
- The Coming of the Antichrist
- Who Hinders These Developments Now?
- When the Restrainer Is Removed
- Jesus Will Destroy the Antichrist
- Recap — The Coming of the Antichrist
- Guarding Against Apostasy

The emphasis of this lesson:

The rapture of the Church is an undeniable doctrine of Scripture. It is the soon-coming return of Jesus, which will supernaturally raise the dead in Christ and gather together the remnant of believers who are alive on the earth, snatching them out of harm's way just in the nick of time.

The times in which we are living are bizarre to say the least. Things are rapidly taking place around us that are absolutely unprecedented. The last of the last days have come. Lawlessness is on the rise and increasing with each passing day. This can only mean the coming of the Lawless One — the Antichrist — is just ahead. But before his debut, another event will take place. It is called *the rapture of the Church*.

If you have ever wondered if there was going to be a rapture of the Church, wonder no more. It is one of the clearest doctrines in the entire New Testament. Paul writes about this cataclysmic event in several of his New Testament epistles — including his letter to the believers in Thessalonica. Here, under the inspiration of the Holy Spirit, Paul wrote:

"For this we say unto you by the word of the Lord, that we which are alive and remain unto the coming of the Lord, shall not prevent them, which are asleep.

"For the Lord himself shall descend from heaven with a shout, with the voice of the archangel, and with the trump of God: and the dead in Christ shall rise first:

"Then we which are alive and remain shall be caught up together with them in the clouds, to meet the Lord in the air: and so shall we ever be with the Lord.

"Wherefore comfort one another with these words."
1 Thessalonians 4:15-18

Let's take a closer look at the meanings of the key words in these verses, beginning with verse 15.

"For this we say unto you by the word of the Lord, that we which are alive and remain unto the coming of the Lord, shall not prevent them, which are asleep."
1 Thessalonians 4:15

There is something quite amazing about reading this passage in the Greek that we cannot receive when reading an English Bible translation. For example, Paul said, "We which are alive and remain." The words "are alive" in Greek are *hoi zontes*, and they describe *the living ones; the vibrant ones*. This phrase refers to those who are *not lifeless and dead*. The word "remain" is *hoi perileipomenoi* in Greek, and it means *the remaining ones; surviving ones; those who are left*, indicating possibly "not many." The word "remain" refers to *a remnant*. This coincides with what is written in Second Thessalonians 2:3, which states that there will be a mass defection from the Christian faith just before the moment of Jesus' return to the earth.

Jesus Himself said, "…When the Son of man cometh, shall he find faith on the earth?" (Luke 18:8) The word "find" here is the Greek word *heurisko*, meaning *to find or discover*. It pictures *a discovery made as a result of careful observance; a moment when one makes a conclusive discovery*. This word usually points to *a discovery made due to intense investigation, scientific study, or scholarly research*. Thus, when Jesus makes His return to gather those who are His own, He will thoroughly investigate and search for people of faith.

Interestingly, the word "faith" in Greek is *ten pistin*. In context, it includes a definite article, which means it actually says *"the faith."* When Jesus begins to carefully observe and intensely investigate the people on the earth at His return, He will find people attending church and observing religious rituals, but finding people who are avidly pursuing "the faith" will be difficult for Him. In other words, there will be such an apostasy in the Church at the time of the rapture that not many will still be spiritually vibrant and alive. Only a *remnant* will be left.

Looking back at First Thessalonians 4:15, it says, "…We which are alive and remain unto the coming of the Lord, shall not prevent them, which are asleep." The word "unto" is the Greek word *eis*, which means *right up to the very moment* of the coming of Christ. The word "coming" is *parousia*, which is *a technical expression for the royal visit of a king or emperor; the arrival of one who alone has the power to deal with a situation*. When Jesus returns, it will be a *parousia* — He's going to come with power to begin putting everything that is in chaos back in order.

Moreover, those who are alive at Christ's coming will "…not prevent them, which are asleep." The words "not prevent" means *will not precede or go before*. The phrase "them which are asleep" in Greek is *tous koimethentas*, which is from the word *koimao*, meaning *to sleep; to sleep deeply; the sleep of death*. It is where we get the words "coma" and "catacomb." Here it describes those who have died having faith in Christ. In God's eyes, they are simply taking a spiritual nap.

Taking into account the original Greek meanings of these words, here is the *Renner Interpretive Version (RIV)* of First Thessalonians 4:15:

> **For we declare this to you by the word of the Lord, those who are physically alive and who have survived everything — I'm talking about the remaining remnant that will still be left around at the time of the coming of the Lord — that living and surviving remnant will not precede those who have already died.**

The apostle Paul goes on to say:

> **For the Lord himself shall descend from heaven with a shout, with the voice of the archangel, and with the trump of God: and the dead in Christ shall rise first.**
> 1 Thessalonians 4:16

Notice it says, "For the Lord himself shall descend...." The word "descend" is the Greek word *katabaino*. It is a compound of *kata*, which means *down*, and the word *baino*, which means *to step; to come down; to move downward from a higher place to a lower place; to descend*. It pictures downward movement with a dominating force. The words "from heaven" in Greek means *directly from the heaven*. Hence, this tells us Christ will swiftly move from His high position in Heaven down toward the earth with a dominating force to begin putting things in order.

A Shout From Jesus: Scripture says when Jesus comes for His Church, He Himself will "shout" as He descends. The word "shout" is the Greek word *keleusma*, and it describes *a direct order or command; a command used to arouse horses, charioteers, hounds, hunters, rowers, masters of ships, etc.* This was a signal given like a trumpet call to muster troops to action. Here we see Christ, the ultimate Commander-in-Chief, calling out and rousing all of Heaven's armies for the gathering of His faithful ones and the final battle of the ages.

The Voice of the Archangel: Accompanied by the mighty shout from Jesus, the Bible also says the Rapture will take place with the "voice of the archangel." The word "voice" is the Greek word *phone*, and it not only describes *a voice, sound, or noise*, but also means *to whirl* and depicts *the sound of wind, wings, or water*. It can also depict *the sound of a massive multitude; an overwhelming sound*.

The Trump of God: Along with the archangel's voice and Jesus' shout will be the "trump of God." In Greek, it is *salpingi Theou*, from the root word *salpingx*, and it depicts *a war trumpet that calls to war; a war trumpet that announces battle and, predictively, ultimate victory and the vanquishing of enemies at the very outset of a military campaign*. This word was used in the Old Testament for moments when God summoned His people to war.

The combination of the overwhelming voice of the archangel, Jesus' shout, and the trump of God will cause "the dead in Christ" to rise again. The phrase "the dead in Christ" in Greek is *hoi nekroi en Christos*, which is from the root word *nekros*, and it describes *a lifeless corpse*. This refers to all believers who have died and are buried in the earth or in the sea. These saints "shall rise first." The phrase "shall rise" is *anastesontai* in Greek, which is from the word *anistemi*, meaning *to stand again; to rise; to be resurrected*. Interestingly this word was also used to depict *a rising of kings and rulers*. Thus, when the dead in Christ are resurrected, they will be raised to rule as royalty with Him in His Kingdom. And they will be "first" to experience this. The word "first" is the Greek word *proton*, which means *first in order; in first place; to begin with*.

Taking into account the original Greek meanings of all these words, here is the *Renner Interpretive Version (RIV)* of First Thessalonians 4:16:

> **For the Lord Himself will descend from Heaven to take charge with a mighty military command that will arouse the saints and galvanize God's troops to action. And along with that command, precisely at that time will also be heard the immense voice of an archangel, along with the blast of God's war trumpet to signal that the final battle, ultimate victory, and vanquishing of all God's enemies is about to occur. That war-trumpet blast will be the indication that God's enemies have lost their longstanding battle with Him and that He reigns victorious and supreme over everyone, over every situation, and over every realm — total victory! And exactly when that war-trumpet sound goes forth, the dead in Christ will immediately stand upright on their feet as they are resurrected to a brand-new, resurrected, royal status. This resurrection will take place as a first priority before the next sequence of events takes place.**

To all this, Paul added:

> **Then we which are alive and remain shall be caught up together with them in the clouds, to meet the Lord in the air: and so shall we ever be with the Lord.**
>
> 1 Thessalonians 4:17

Immediately after the resurrection of the dead in Christ, the rapture of those alive in Christ will occur. The word "then" in verse 17 is the Greek word *epeita*, which means *upon that moment; exactly at that moment; exactly then*. To this Paul added the same exact phrase he used in verse 15: "we which are alive and remain." This phrase in Greek is *hoi zontes*, and it means *the living ones; to be alive, not lifeless and dead*. These are the believers who have survived everything that has taken place up until that point and have not fallen away into apostasy. The Bible says they "remain," which in Greek means *the remaining ones; surviving ones; those who are left*, and it indicates possibly not many. What Paul is telling us here is that when Christ returns for the Church, there may only be a small remnant of spiritually vibrant Christians left.

Nevertheless, this remnant of rapture-ready believers will be "caught up together" with the dead in Christ who have been resurrected. The phrase "caught up together" is the Greek word *harpagesometha*, which is a form of the word *harpadzo*, and it means *to catch, seize, or take away; to snatch suddenly*. It carries the idea of *snatching someone out of danger just in time*. This tells us that the rapture of the Church will occur in a dangerous moment. When things seem to look ominously perilous for believers, Christ is going to come suddenly and snatch us out of danger just in the nick of time.

The Bible says we will "meet the Lord in the air." The word "meet" is *apantesis* in Greek, and it means *to the meeting; to the reception; to the encounter*. It is a technical word used for *the reception of a newly arrived official or royalty*. In other words, when we meet Jesus in the air, He is going to roll out the red carpet for us! He is going to give us a VIP reception, and it's going to be grand!

The word "air" is a Greek word that describes *the lower regions of the heavens; the lower atmosphere*. So as Christ gives a shout and the archangel voices His arrival, the Lord will descend from Heaven into the lower regions of the atmosphere. His shout will galvanize the angelic troops and resurrect the dead in Christ, and the Lord Himself will seize and snatch us away from imminent danger. It will be a VIP reception, and from then on, we will "ever be with the Lord." In Greek, the phrase "ever be" is *pantote*, and it indicates *at all times; all the time; always; continually; perpetually*.

Putting together the original Greek meanings of all these words in all three verses, here is the *Renner Interpretive Version (RIV)* of First Thessalonians 4:15-17:

> **For we declare this to you by the word of the Lord, those who are physically alive and who have survived everything — I'm talking about the remaining remnant that will still be left around at the time of the coming of the Lord — that living and surviving remnant will not precede those who have already died.**
>
> **For the Lord Himself will descend from Heaven to take charge with a mighty military command that will arouse the saints and galvanize God's troops to action. And along with that command, precisely at that time will also be heard the immense voice of an archangel, along with the blast of God's war trumpet**

to signal that the final battle, ultimate victory, and vanquishing of all God's enemies is about to occur. That war-trumpet blast will be the indication that God's enemies have lost their longstanding battle with Him and that He reigns victorious and supreme over everyone, over every situation, and over every realm — total victory! And exactly when that war-trumpet sound goes forth, the dead in Christ will immediately stand upright on their feet as they are resurrected to a brand-new, resurrected, royal status. This resurrection will take place as a first priority before the next sequence of events takes place.

Then at that exact synchronized moment, those who are still physically alive and who have survived everything — I'm talking about the remnant that will still be around and left remaining at this time — they will suddenly and supernaturally be snatched away out of imminent danger just in the nick of time as the Lord instigates a divine rescue operation to transport them into the clouds to join those who have been resurrected. There in the air's lower atmosphere where the Lord has descended to meet them, those who were raised from the dead and the remnant who were supernaturally snatched out of danger, will encounter the Lord. And at that encounter, the Lord will roll out the red carpet to give the new arrivals a royal reception to match the VIP status He knows they deserve! Then and after that, we will always — at all times and forevermore — be with the Lord.

Isn't that amazing! In our next lesson, we will take a close look at First Corinthians 15:51 and 52 to see what the Bible says about the changes our physical bodies will undergo at the time of the rapture.

STUDY QUESTIONS

> Study to shew thyself approved unto God, a workman that needeth not to be ashamed, rightly dividing the word of truth.
> — 2 Timothy 2:15

1. Prior to this teaching, what did you know and understand about the rapture of the Church?

2. How has this lesson expanded your grasp on the subject? What new things have you learned regarding…
   - The sequence of the rapture events?
   - The *shout* from Jesus, the *voice* of the archangel, and the *trump of God*?
   - The meaning of "caught up together" with them "to meet the Lord in the air"?

PRACTICAL APPLICATION

> But be ye doers of the word, and not hearers only, deceiving your own selves.
> —James 1:22

1. What are you most excited about and looking forward to regarding the rapture?
2. The Bible tells us that when Christ returns for the Church, there may only be a small remnant of spiritually vibrant Christians left. What does this say to you personally about being ready?
3. Is there anything specific you feel you need to deal with right now to prepare yourself for His coming? Are there any attitudes, actions, or ways of thinking you need to repent of and ask God to help you change?

LESSON 2

TOPIC

In the Twinkling of an Eye

SCRIPTURES

1. **1 Corinthians 15:51,52** — Behold, I shew you a mystery; We shall not all sleep, but we shall all be changed, in a moment, in the twinkling of an eye, at the last trump: for the trumpet shall sound, and the dead shall be raised incorruptible, and we shall be changed.

GREEK WORDS

1. "behold" — ἰδού (*idou*): bewilderment, shock, amazement, and wonder
2. "I shew" — λέγω (*lego*): "I say," not show; mysteries are revealed by speech
3. "mystery" — μυστήριον (*musterion*): a mystery; a secret; a secret once hidden, but now revealed
4. "sleep" — κοιμηθησόμεθα (*koimethesometha*): from κοιμάω (*koimao*); to sleep; to sleep deeply; the sleep of death; death; where we get the words "coma" and "catacomb"
5. "shall… be changed" — ἀλλαγησόμεθα (*allagesometha*): to change; to exchange one thing for another; to transform
6. "moment" — ἄτομος (*atomos*): an indivisible moment; a split second; an instant; where we get the word "atom"; something tiny or microscopic
7. "twinkling" — ῥιπή (*rhipe*): twinkling; twitch; so fast it is almost undetectable
8. "trump" — σάλπιγξ (*salpingx*): depicts a war trumpet; a war trumpet that boldly announces victory and the vanquishing of His enemies at the outset of a military campaign; prophetically depicts that moment when a trumpet was blasted to instigate war and to declare intended triumph and victory even at the outset of a war campaign; used in the Old Testament for moments when God summoned His people to war
9. "dead" — νεκρός (*nekros*): a lifeless corpse; a cadaver with no life left in it; plural, "corpses"
10. "incorruptible" — ἄφθαρτος (*aphthartos*): something that is incapable of decay; that which is incapable of suffering the effects of wear, tear, and age; timeless, immortal, indestructible
11. "shall be changed" — ἀλλαγησόμεθα (*allagesometha*): to change; to exchange one thing for another; to transform

SYNOPSIS

When Jesus talked about His return, He said, "But about that day or hour no one knows, not even the angels in heaven, nor the Son, but only the Father. Be on guard! Be alert! You do not know when that time will come" (Mark 13:32,33 *NIV*). Just as Jesus really came to the earth in the past, He has promised to come again in the future. The rapture of the Church is real! It will happen fast and without warning. The question is, are you ready for it?

The emphasis of this lesson:
All the events of the rapture of the Church will take place in the twinkling of an eye. The dead in Christ will be raised to incorruptible, everlasting life, and the remnant of believers alive on the earth will be caught up into the air and transformed into immortal, indestructible beings.

A Review of First Thessalonians 4:15-17

Before we dive into our second lesson, let's briefly review what we've learned so far about the rapture of the Church. Taking into account the original Greek meanings of the words found in this passage, here is the *Renner Interpretive Version (RIV)* of First Thessalonians 4:15:

> **For we declare this to you by the word of the Lord, those who are physically alive and who have survived everything — I'm talking about the remaining remnant that will still be left around at the time of the coming of the Lord — that living and surviving remnant will not precede those who have already died.**

In First Thessalonians 4:16, the apostle Paul went on to say, "For the Lord himself shall descend from heaven with a shout, with the voice of the archangel, and with the trump of God: and the dead in Christ shall rise first." We saw that the word "shout" in Greek is *keleusma*, a specific word used to describe *a commander who gave a shout to muster together and galvanize all the troops for battle.* This shout was always a declaration that war was commencing and it was the guarantee that in the end, this commander would be the supreme victor.

Taking into account the original Greek meanings of all the words found in this passage, here is the *Renner Interpretive Version (RIV)* of First Thessalonians 4:16:

> **For the Lord Himself will descend from Heaven to take charge with a mighty military command that will arouse the saints and galvanize God's troops to action. And along with that command, precisely at that time will also be heard the immense**

voice of an archangel, along with the blast of God's war trumpet to signal that the final battle, ultimate victory, and vanquishing of all God's enemies is about to occur. That war-trumpet blast will be the indication that God's enemies have lost their longstanding battle with Him and that He reigns victorious and supreme over everyone, over every situation, and over every realm — total victory! And exactly when that war-trumpet sound goes forth, the dead in Christ will immediately stand upright on their feet as they are resurrected to a brand-new, resurrected, royal status. This resurrection will take place as a first priority before the next sequence of events takes place.

What will happen next? First Thessalonians 4:17 says, "Then we which are alive and remain shall be caught up together with them in the clouds, to meet the Lord in the air: and so shall we ever be with the Lord." We learned in Lesson 1 that the word "then" is the Greek word *epeita*, which means *upon that moment; exactly at that moment; exactly then*. So as soon as the dead in Christ are raised to life, the next immediate rapture-related event in the sequence is for those who "are alive and remain" to be caught up together with them in the clouds. In Greek, the words "are alive" describe *the living ones* — those who are still *spiritually vibrant*. The implication is that many who were once alive will be spiritually asleep when Christ returns.

The Bible describes these *living ones* that are *spiritually awake* as those who "remain." In Greek, the word for "remain" describes *the remnant of a garment*. This word could be translated as *remaining ones* or *surviving ones*, indicating possibly not many. Because of a massive defection from the Christian faith — or a great "falling away" as Second Thessalonians 2:3 describes it — there will only be a small remnant of spiritually alive people. Nonetheless, these vibrant ones will be "caught up together" in the air with the resurrected saints.

"Caught up together" is a compound of the words *apo*, meaning *away*, and *harpadzo*, which means *to seize or to snatch out of danger just in the nick of time*. The use of this word indicates that believers who are alive on the earth will be surrounded by extreme difficulty just before Christ returns. In that moment, He will descend from Heaven with a commanding, dominating force and grab us out of the natural realm and pull us into the supernatural realm. And we will meet the Lord in the air.

"**Meet**" in Greek is *apantesis*, which is a technical word used for *the reception of newly arrived officials, dignitaries, or royalty*. The Holy Spirit prompted Paul to use this word to let us know that when Jesus snatches us out of danger, He is going to roll out the red carpet and give us a grand, VIP reception! And this will all take place in the "air," which is a Greek word describing *the lower regions of the atmosphere*. Once we are together with Jesus, we will "ever be" with Him. The phrase "ever be" is the Greek word *pantote*, which means *at all times; all the time; always; continually; or perpetually*.

Taking into account the original Greek meanings of all the words found in this passage, here is the *Renner Interpretive Version (RIV)* of First Thessalonians 4:17:

> **Then at that exact synchronized moment, those who are still physically alive and who have survived everything — I'm talking about the remnant that will still be around and left remaining at this time — they will suddenly and supernaturally be snatched away out of imminent danger just in the nick of time as the Lord instigates a divine rescue operation to transport them into the clouds to join those who have been resurrected. There in the air's lower atmosphere where the Lord has descended to meet them, those who were raised from the dead and the remnant who were supernaturally snatched out of danger, will encounter the Lord. And at that encounter, the Lord will roll out the red carpet to give the new arrivals a royal reception to match the VIP status He knows they deserve! Then and after that, we will always — at all times and forevermore — be with the Lord**

'Behold, I shew you a mystery'

Through the apostle Paul, the Holy Spirit wrote First Corinthians 15:51 and 52, giving us more details of what we can expect to take place at the time of the rapture. It says:

> "Behold, I shew you a mystery; We shall not all sleep, but we shall all be changed, in a moment, in the twinkling of an eye, at the last trump: for the trumpet shall sound, and the dead shall be raised incorruptible, and we shall be changed."

Notice the word "behold," which Paul chose to begin verse 51. It is the Greek word *idou*, and it describes *bewilderment, shock, amazement, and wonder*. What Paul was about to say was so magnificent and so dumbfounding, he was left speechless. He paused in awe and said, "Wow!" Think about it. Paul was about to describe the resurrection of the dead and the rapture of the Church — something the Lord Himself had revealed to him.

Next Paul said, "I shew you a mystery." The phrase "I shew" is the Greek word *lego*, which means "I say." Mysteries are revealed by speech, not by showing something. As Paul spoke in his letter, he was unveiling a "mystery." The word "mystery" is the Greek word *musterion*, and it describes *a mystery; a secret; a secret that was once hidden, but now is revealed*. What is this mystery that was hidden? It is the mystery of the rapture of the Church!

'We shall not all sleep, but we shall all be changed'

Paul wrote, "…We shall not all sleep, but we shall all be changed" (1 Corinthians 15:51). The word "sleep" here is similar to the word "asleep" in First Thessalonians 4:15. It is the Greek word *koimethesometha*, which is from the word *koimao*, meaning *to sleep* or *to sleep deeply*. It is the word for *death* or *the sleep of death*, and it is where we get the words "coma" and "catacomb." Paul was telling believers — both then and now — that not every believer is going to die. There will be one generation of loyal Christ followers in the last of the last days that will not see death.

He said that generation "shall all be changed," which in Greek means *to change* or *to exchange one thing for another*. It is the same word that means *to transform*. The use of this word tells us that the remnant of believers who are alive when Jesus returns are going to be snatched up suddenly into the lower atmosphere, and they will exchange their physical earthly bodies for a new kind of body. This exchange will be a miraculous, supernatural transformation.

Taking into account the original Greek meanings of all these words, here is the *Renner Interpretive Version (RIV)* of First Corinthians 15:51:

> **What I am about to say will totally flabbergast you, but listen carefully, for I am going to tell you something that was previously an unknown mystery, but has now been revealed to us. Here it is: All will not die, but all — the dead and even the**

living — will be altered, changed, miraculously modified, and transformed.

'In the twinkling of an eye'

In First Corinthians 15:52, Paul went on to tell us how that transformation will take place. He said, "In a moment, in the twinkling of an eye, at the last trump: for the trumpet shall sound, and the dead shall be raised incorruptible, and we shall be changed." Let's unpack the meaning of the key words in this verse, starting with the word "moment."

In Greek, the word "moment" is *atomos*, and it describes *an indivisible moment; a split second; an instant.* This is where we get the word "atom." It indicates *something tiny or microscopic.* The use of the word *atomos* tells us the transformation is going to happen so fast, it will be virtually impossible to detect with the human eye.

To this, Paul added the phrase "twinkling of an eye." The word "twinkling" is the Greek word *rhipe*, which describes *a twinkling or a twitch*. It is *something so fast it is almost undetectable*. One of the best examples to illustrate this word is the twitching of one's eye. If you have ever experienced an eye twitch, you have an idea of the velocity of "twinkling." It comes and goes so fast, an outside observer can barely see it. That's how fast the remnant of believers and the dead in Christ will be raptured and their bodies transformed.

'At the last trump'

When will our rapid transformation take place? Paul said, "at the last trump." The Greek word for "trump" here happens to be the exact same word for "trump" that appears in First Thessalonians 4:16. It is the word *salpingx*, and it depicts *a war trumpet that boldly announces victory and the vanquishing of one's enemies at the outset of a military campaign.* Prophetically, this word indicates that moment when a trumpet was blasted to instigate war and to declare intended triumph and victory even at the outset of a war campaign. It was used in the Old Testament for moments when God summoned His people to war.

Friends, what Paul was talking about here is the moment when Jesus descends from Heaven into the air's lower atmosphere and He gives a shout to announce that the last battle is about to begin. His shout will muster together the angelic troops and galvanize all the saints in the earth.

In this *atomos* moment of time, the Church will be raptured and the seven-year timer for the great tribulation will be started. This final battle will be massive, but the sounding of this last trump is a declarative guarantee of Jesus' victory! When the seven years of utter turmoil are complete, He will return to the earth once more as the King of kings and the Lord of lords! This is the Second Coming of Christ.

'The dead shall be raised incorruptible, and we shall be changed'

First Corinthians 15:52 goes on to say, "…for the trumpet shall sound, and the dead shall be raised incorruptible, and we shall be changed." Here again we see a similar description of what Paul stated in First Thessalonians 4:16 and 17. The word "dead" is the Greek word *nekros*, which describes *a lifeless corpse; a cadaver with no life left in it*. In this case, it is plural, "corpses." In light of First Thessalonians 4:16, we know this refers to "the dead in Christ."

Scripture says the believers who have already died will be raised "incorruptible," which is the Greek word *aphthartos*, and it describes *something that is incapable of decay; that which is incapable of suffering the effects of wear, tear, and age*. The word "incorruptible" actually defines how our physical bodies "shall be changed." We will exchange our temporary, mortal bodies for timeless, immortal, and indestructible ones. And all this will take place in a moment, in the twinkling of an eye at the time of the rapture.

Taking into account the original Greek meanings of all these words, here is the *Renner Interpretive Version (RIV)* of First Corinthians 15:52:

> **In a moment — a split second, an indivisible atom of time — as fast as the twitch of an eye, at the very last trump, that war trumpet will loudly sound to signal that the final battle, ultimate victory, and vanquishing of all God's enemies is about to finally happen. That blast will be God's way of letting everyone know that His enemies have lost their footing and longstanding battle with Him and that He reigns victorious and supreme in total victory!**
>
> **In that flash, the dead will stand upright on their feet and will be resurrected to a brand-new, resurrected, royal status. And at that exact moment, they will miraculously receive new bodies**

that are incapable of decay and that will never again show the effects of wear, tear, and age — timeless, immortal, indestructible bodies. We who are still alive when all this happens will be supernaturally transformed as our old bodies are exchanged for new ones that also are incapable of decay and that will never again show the effects of wear, tear, and age. Our bodies will literally be altered, changed, miraculously modified, and transformed into timeless, immortal, indestructible bodies.

Friend, that is what is ahead in your future! It is the blessed hope of life eternal with Jesus. In our next lesson, we will pull back the curtains of time and catch a glimpse of the very end of the age just before the Antichrist makes his debut.

STUDY QUESTIONS

> Study to shew thyself approved unto God, a workman that needeth not to be ashamed, rightly dividing the word of truth.
> — 2 Timothy 2:15

1. What new details about the rapture did you learn from First Corinthians 15:51 and 52?

2. What connections is the Holy Spirit showing you between Paul's words in First Thessalonians 4:15-17 and First Corinthians 15:51 and 52?

3. It appears that when Jesus returns to rapture the Church, many will be spiritually asleep. According to these verses, what can you do to stay spiritually awake and vibrant?
   - Matthew 26:41; Mark 14:38
   - Luke 12:35-40; Revelation 16:15
   - Romans 13:11-14

PRACTICAL APPLICATION

> But be ye doers of the word, and not hearers only, deceiving your own selves.
> — James 1:22

1. How does the thought of exchanging your physical earthly body for a new kind of heavenly body encourage you?
2. Have you ever looked at the rapture as a "divine rescue operation" led by the Lord? How does this perspective influence your thinking?
3. Is there anything you are involved in that is causing you to be spiritually drowsy? If so, what is it, and what steps can you take to disengage from this activity?

LESSON 3

TOPIC

Beware of Inaccurate Prophecy Teachers

SCRIPTURES

1. **1 Corinthians 15:51,52** — Behold, I shew you a mystery; We shall not all sleep, but we shall all be changed, in a moment, in the twinkling of an eye, at the last trump: for the trumpet shall sound, and the dead shall be raised incorruptible, and we shall be changed.
2. **2 Thessalonians 2:1,2** — Now we beseech you, brethren, by the coming of our Lord Jesus Christ, and by our gathering together unto him, that ye be not soon shaken in mind, or be troubled, neither by spirit, nor by word, nor by letter as from us, as that the day of Christ is at hand.

GREEK WORDS

1. "moment" — ἄτομος (*atomos*): an indivisible moment; a split second; an instant; where we get the word "atom"; something tiny or microscopic
2. "twinkling" — ῥιπή (*rhipe*): twinkling; twitch; so fast it is almost undetectable
3. "trump" — σάλπιγξ (*salpingx*): depicts a war trumpet; a war trumpet that boldly announces victory and the vanquishing of His enemies at the outset of a military campaign; prophetically depicts that moment when a trumpet was blasted to instigate war and to declare intended

triumph and victory even at the outset of a war campaign; used in the Old Testament for moments when God summoned His people to war

4. "beseech" — ἐρωτάω (*erotao*): an earnest request by someone with a preferred position; to request with the expectation that the request will be heard, honored, obeyed, or satisfied
5. "coming" — παρουσία (*parousia*): indicates that moment when Christ comes to collect His people at the end of the age
6. "gathering together" — ἐπισυναγωγή (*episunagoge*): a gathering together
7. "soon" — ταχέως (*tacheos*): swift; fast; to do something as swiftly as possible
8. "shaken" — σαλεύω (*saleuo*): to shake, to waver, to totter; or to be moved; the tense points to events that cause shock or alarm; refers to an event or repeated events so unexpected that it results in shock or distress; worry and inward anxiety resulting from outward events that keep occurring repeatedly, as if there is no pause between shocking, debilitating, and nerve-racking happenings; one scholar translates it as jumpiness or nervousness
9. "mind" — νοῦς (*nous*): mind, will, emotions
10. "troubled" — θροέω (*throeo*): inward fright that causes one to be filled with worry, anxiety, or fear; tense points to an ongoing state of worry and inward anxiety resulting from outward events that keep occurring repeatedly, as if there is no pause between these shocking, debilitating, and nerve-racking happenings; hence, jumpiness or nervousness
11. "by spirit" — διὰ πνεύματος (*dia pneumatos*): from πνεῦμα (*pneuma*), which means "spirit" in this verse; as used here, refers to a spiritual experience or spiritual utterance that is out of sync with the revealed Word of God; some translate it as ecstatic utterances; here, it refers to strange utterances, weird revelations, or euphoric proclamations that have no root in sound doctrine and eventually produce the negative effect of spiritually upsetting the Church
12. "by word" — διὰ λόγου (*dia logou*): by word; by rumor; by verbal claim
13. "letter" — ἐπιστολή (*epistole*): letter; epistle

SYNOPSIS

In our last lesson, we took a close look at what the Bible says is going to happen to our physical bodies at the time of the rapture. The apostle Paul talked about this in First Corinthians 1:51 and 52, which says, "Behold, I shew you a mystery; We shall not all sleep, but we shall all be changed, in a moment, in the twinkling of an eye, at the last trump: for the trumpet shall sound, and the dead shall be raised incorruptible, and we shall be changed."

We saw that the word "moment" in Greek is *atomos*, and it describes *an indivisible moment; a split second; an instant.* It is where we get the word "atom," and it depicts *something tiny or microscopic.* The word "twinkling" in Greek is *rhipe*, which denotes *a twinkling or a twitch; something so fast it is almost undetectable.* If you have ever experienced an eye twitch, you know how fast a twinkling takes place.

The Bible goes on to say these things will occur "at the last trump." The Greek word for "trump" in First Corinthians 15:52 is the same one used in First Thessalonians 4:16. It is the word *salpingx*, and it depicts *a war trumpet that boldly announces victory and the vanquishing of one's enemies at the outset of a military campaign.* Prophetically, it denotes the moment when a trumpet was blasted to instigate war and to declare intended triumph and victory even at the outset of a war campaign. Thus, when Jesus comes and the last trumpet is sounded, He will be declaring war against the rebellious residents of the world and the demonic spirits working through them.

Taking into account the original Greek meanings of all the key words in these verses, here is the *Renner Interpretive Version (RIV)* of First Corinthians 15:51 and 52:

> **What I am about to say will totally flabbergast you, but listen carefully, for I am going to tell you something that was previously an unknown mystery, but has now been revealed to us. Here it is: All will not die, but all — the dead and even the living — will be altered, changed, miraculously modified, and transformed.**
>
> **In a moment — a split second, an indivisible atom of time — as fast as the twitch of an eye, at the very last trump, that war trumpet will loudly sound to signal that the final battle, ultimate victory, and vanquishing of all God's enemies is about to**

finally happen. That blast will be God's way of letting everyone know that His enemies have lost their footing and longstanding battle with Him and that He reigns victorious and supreme in total victory!

In that flash, the dead will stand upright on their feet and will be resurrected to a brand-new, resurrected, royal status. And at that exact moment, they will miraculously receive new bodies that are incapable of decay and that will never again show the effects of wear, tear, and age — timeless, immortal, indestructible bodies. We who are still alive when all this happens will be supernaturally transformed as our old bodies are exchanged for new ones that also are incapable of decay and that will never again show the effects of wear, tear, and age. Our bodies will literally be altered, changed, miraculously modified, and transformed into timeless, immortal, indestructible bodies.

The emphasis of this lesson:

There are many outrageous and unnerving events that are going to happen in rapid succession just before the rapture of the Church. God wants us to keep our eyes focused on Jesus, our hearts and minds filled with His Word, and our ears closed to inaccurate teachers who are out of sync with Scripture.

Don't Listen to Inaccurate Prophecy Teachers

In addition to the apostle Paul talking about the rapture of the Church in First Thessalonians 4:15-17, he also discussed it in Second Thessalonians 2:1 and 2. He said:

> "Now we beseech you, brethren, by the coming of our Lord Jesus Christ, and by our gathering together unto him, that ye be not soon shaken in mind, or be troubled, neither by spirit, nor by word, nor by letter as from us, as that the day of Christ is at hand."

It is important to note that Paul wrote these verses to the Thessalonian believers because they had begun to listen to inaccurate prophecy teachers who were claiming that the rapture had already taken place. These believers were young in their faith, and when they heard that Christ had already returned, they were afraid they had been left behind. (Just imagine how fearful you would be if you thought you had missed the Rapture.)

Paul said, "Now we beseech you, brethren." The word "beseech" is the Greek word *erotao*, which describes *an earnest request by someone with a preferred position*. Such a request came with the expectation that the request would be heard, honored, obeyed, or satisfied. Basically, this is a picture of Paul pulling rank on the new believers. He was telling them to listen carefully and obey fully what he was about to say.

The Rapture and Christ's Second Coming Are Two Different Events

He then mentioned "the coming of our Lord Jesus Christ." In Greek, the word "coming" is *parousia*, which indicates *that moment when Christ comes to collect His people at the end of the age*. What's interesting about the word *parousia* is that it is most often used to describe the second coming of Christ — not the rapture of the Church. These are actually two different events that take place separately.

The rapture occurs at the end of the Church age — the period in which we are now living. The second coming of Christ will take place at the end of the seven-year tribulation. Jude, one of Jesus' brothers, referred to this in his book, saying, "…Behold, the Lord cometh with ten thousands of his saints, to execute judgement upon all…" (Jude 1:14,15). After the seven-year tribulation, Christ will come and deal with all of His enemies and put things in order. We will be among the multitude of saints when He returns to set up His millennial reign.

Although Paul used the word *parousia* interchangeably in his writings to describe the second coming of Christ and the rapture of the Church, in Second Thessalonians 2:1, he was referring to the Rapture. The reason we know this to be the case is because of the words that immediately follow it. He said, "Now we beseech you, brethren, by the coming (*parousia*) of our Lord Jesus Christ, and by our gathering together unto him."

Notice the words "gathering together." This is a clear reference to the Rapture. It is the Greek term *episunagoge*, which describes a moment in the future when the Lord will quickly gather together His people to Himself at the end of the age.

Taking into account the original Greek meanings of the words in this verse, here is the *Renner Interpretive Version (RIV)* of Second Thessalonians 2:1:

> **Brothers, listen carefully, for I am asking you in the strongest of terms to hear what I am about to say and to do exactly what I'm asking you to do. The appearance of the Lord Jesus Christ is very near. The moment we have all longed and waited for is almost upon us! I'm talking about that moment when Jesus will finally gather us together for Himself.**

'Be Not Soon Shaken'

To this Paul added, "That ye be not soon shaken…" (2 Thessalonians 2:2). Again, he wrote this to the believers in Thessalonica because they were listening to prophecy teachers that were teaching error. Specifically, they claimed that Jesus had already returned to rapture His Church, and the Thessalonians had missed it.

In order to dispel the lie and calm their fears, Paul said, "…Be not soon shaken…." The word "soon" is the Greek word *tacheos*, which means *swift or fast; to do something as swiftly as possible*. And the word "shaken" is the Greek word *saleuo*, meaning *to shake; to waver, to totter; or to be moved*. By using this word, Paul was saying, "Don't be shaken! Don't totter or waver or be quickly moved by what you're hearing from others."

Equally important here is the tense of the word *saleuo* — translated here as "shaken." It points to *events that cause shock or alarm*. Moreover, it refers to *an event or repeated events so unexpected that it results in shock or distress, worry, and inward anxiety*. These outward events keep occurring repeatedly, as if there is no pause between the shocking, debilitating, and nerve-racking happenings. One scholar translates the word *saleuo* ("shaken") as *jumpiness* or *nervousness*.

By using this word, the apostle Paul was informing us that as we get closer and closer to the end of the age, it's going to be as if there's no pause between all the unbelievable happenings in society and in the world around us. This is confirmed by Jesus' teaching on the end of the age in Matthew 24:8 (*NIV*), which says, "All these are the beginning of birth pains."

Think about it. A woman who is in labor and about to give birth begins to have contractions. The closer she gets to the delivery, the closer and closer the contractions become — and the more intense they are — until finally it's nearly one contraction on top of another. That is exactly what the tense in this verse describes. Paul urged the Thessalonian believers — and us — not to be shaken by outward events that keep happening repeatedly, over and over, almost without pause between them.

Don't Believe Everything You See and Hear

Interestingly, Paul specifically said, "…Be not soon shaken in mind…" (2 Thessalonians 2:2). The word "mind" here is the Greek word *nous*, which is essentially *a person's mind, will, and emotions*. Paul was warning them not to be perpetually jumpy or nervous in their soul.

He went on to say, "…or be troubled, neither by spirit, nor by word, nor by letter as from us, as that the day of Christ is at hand" (2 Thessalonians 2:2). The word "troubled" in Greek is the word *throeo*, and it describes *an inward fright that causes one to be filled with worry, anxiety, or fear*. Again, just as with the word *saleuo* ("shaken"), the tense of the word *throeo* ("troubled") points to *an ongoing state of worry and inward anxiety resulting from outward events that keep occurring repeatedly*, as if there is no pause between these shocking, debilitating, and nerve-racking happenings.

When Paul said the words "neither by spirit," he used the Greek phrase *dia pneumatos*, which is from the word *pneuma*, meaning "spirit." In this verse, the phrase *dia pneumatos* refers to *a spiritual experience* or *spiritual utterance that is out of sync with the revealed Word of God*. Some scholars translate it as *ecstatic utterances*, but here it refers *to strange utterances, weird revelations, or euphoric proclamations* that have no root in sound doctrine and eventually produce the negative effect of spiritually upsetting the Church. In context, Paul was saying, "Don't become perpetually anxious and worried by something that appears to be prophecy, but it really isn't." In other words, "Don't believe every prophecy you hear."

Paul also cautioned them not to be troubled "by word." In Greek, this is the word *dia logou*, and it means *by word; by rumor; by verbal claim*. This would best be described as *the latest rumor*. Basically, Paul was saying, "Don't believe every conspiracy theory or rumor that comes your way." If you believe everything you read or hear on the Internet and on the news, you will be frantically upset from daylight till dark. Speaking through

Paul, the Holy Spirit is telling all believers everywhere to shut our ears to this nonsense.

Lastly, Paul warned the Thessalonian believers not to be shaken in mind or troubled "…by letter as from us, as that the day of Christ is at hand" (2 Thessalonians 2:2). The word "letter" in Greek is *epistole*, and it literally means *letter* or *epistle*. Apparently, there were fraudulent people moving about in Paul's day who were writing letters to believers that were similar in style and verse to his, but they were written with wrong motives. Some of these individuals even claimed to have Paul's endorsement, while others went so far as to say the letter was written by Paul himself, but it wasn't.

In Second Thessalonians 2:2, we see that someone had written a letter to the new believers at Thessalonica claiming that the rapture of the Church had already taken place. If true, it meant the Thessalonian believers had missed it. To calm their fears, Paul basically said, "Don't be shaken or troubled by such nonsense."

Taking into account the original Greek meanings of the words in this verse, here is the *Renner Interpretive Version (RIV)* of Second Thessalonians 2:2:

> **Some things will be happening right before His coming that could shake you up quite a bit. I'm referring to events that will be so dramatic that they could leave your head spinning — occurrences of such a serious nature that many people will end up feeling alarmed, panicked, intimidated, and unnerved. Naturally speaking, these events could put your nerves on edge and make you feel apprehensive and insecure. How I wish I could tell you these incidents were going to be just a one-shot deal, but when they finally get rolling, they're going to keep coming and coming, one after another. That's why you have to determine not to be shaken or moved by anything you see or hear. You need to get a grip on your mind and refuse to allow yourselves to be traumatized by these events. If you let these things get to you, it won't be too long until you're a nervous wreck! That's why you have to decide beforehand that you are not going to give in and allow fright to penetrate its way into your mind and emotions until it runs your whole life. I also want to tell you not to be too surprised if people start making weird spiritual proclamations and off-the-wall utterances**

during the time just before the Lord comes. All kinds of strange things are going to happen during those days! It's going to get so bizarre that you might even receive a letter from some person who claims that the day of the Lord has already come! Who knows — he might even attach our name to it, alleging to have our endorsement. Or he might even send it as if it were written and sent from us

In our next lesson, we will focus our attention on what the Bible says about the Antichrist in Second Thessalonians 2:3 and how he will step onto the world's stage in the near future.

STUDY QUESTIONS

> Study to shew thyself approved unto God, a workman that needeth not to be ashamed, rightly dividing the word of truth.
> — 2 Timothy 2:15

1. In your own words, explain the difference between the *rapture of the Church* and *the second coming of Christ*.
2. God doesn't want you to blindly believe everything you see and hear. Carefully read First John 4:1-6 and First Thessalonians 5:21 and 22, and identify what He wants you to do.
3. If a word of prophecy or wisdom is truly from God, what kind of effects will it produce in your life and the lives of others? (Consider Galatians 5:22,23; James 3:17.)

PRACTICAL APPLICATION

> But be ye doers of the word, and not hearers only, deceiving your own selves.
> — James 1:22

1. The believers in Thessalonica were young in the faith, and when they heard that Christ had already returned, they were afraid they had been *left behind*. How do you think you would respond if you had just heard that the rapture had taken place and you missed it?
2. If you knew for a fact that Jesus Christ was returning to rapture the Church at some point within the next six months, how would you

live differently? What would you *stop* doing, and what would you *start* doing? What is keeping you from making these adjustments now?

3. In Second Thessalonians 2:2, Paul informed us that as we get closer and closer to the end of the age, it's going to be as if there's no pause between all the unbelievable happenings in the world around us. In what specific ways would you say this verse is already taking place today?

LESSON 4

TOPIC
A Worldwide Mutiny Against God's Standards

SCRIPTURES
1. **2 Thessalonians 2:1-3** — Now we beseech you, brethren, by the coming of our Lord Jesus Christ, and by our gathering together unto him, that ye be not soon shaken in mind, or be troubled, neither by spirit, nor by word, nor by letter as from us, as that the day of Christ is at hand. Let no man deceive you by any means: for that day shall not come, except there come a falling away first, and that man of sin be revealed, the son of perdition.

GREEK WORDS
1. "beseech" — ἐρωτάω (*erotao*): an earnest request by someone with a preferred position; to request with the expectation that the request will be heard, honored, obeyed, or satisfied
2. "coming" — παρουσία (*parousia*): indicates that moment when Christ comes to collect His people at the end of the age
3. "gathering together" — ἐπισυναγωγή (*episunagoge*): a gathering together
4. "soon" — ταχέως (*tacheos*): swift; fast; to do something as swiftly as possible
5. "shaken" — σαλεύω (*saleuo*): to shake, to waver, to totter; or to be moved; the tense points to events that cause shock or alarm; refers to

an event or repeated events so unexpected that it results in shock or distress; worry and inward anxiety resulting from outward events that keep occurring repeatedly, as if there is no pause between shocking, debilitating, and nerve-racking happenings; one scholar translates it as jumpiness or nervousness

6. "mind" — νοῦς (*nous*): mind, will, emotions
7. "troubled" — θροέω (*throeo*): inward fright that causes one to be filled with worry, anxiety, or fear; tense points to an ongoing state of worry and inward anxiety resulting from outward events that keep occurring repeatedly, as if there is no pause between these shocking, debilitating, and nerve-racking happenings; hence, jumpiness or nervousness
8. "by spirit" — διὰ πνεύματος (*dia pneumatos*): from πνεῦμα (*pneuma*), which means "spirit" in this verse; as used here, refers to a spiritual experience or spiritual utterance that is out of sync with the revealed Word of God; some translate it as ecstatic utterances; here, it refers to strange utterances, weird revelations, or euphoric proclamations that have no root in sound doctrine and eventually produce the negative effect of spiritually upsetting the Church
9. "by word" — διὰ λόγου (*dia logou*): by word; by rumor; by verbal claim
10. "by letter" — ἐπιστολή (*epistole*): letter; epistle
11. "no man" — μή τις (*me tis*): denotes a strong prohibition, sternly and strongly ordering the reader to reject some type of activity
12. "deceive" — ἐξαπατάω (*exapatao*): cheat; seduce; to take advantage of by trickery; to deceive by giving distorted impressions; to lure one into deception; using any means to promote delusional thinking and believing
13. "by any means" — κατὰ μηδένα τρόπον (*kata medena tropon*): in no way at all; in no fashion; "don't give them an inch"; refuse to let them dominate you with their manipulations
14. "falling away" — ἀποστασία (*apostasia*): a falling away or revolt; describes political revolt; a mutiny
15. "first" — πρῶτον (*proton*): first in order; in first place; to begin with
16. "sin" — ἀνομία (*anomia*): lawlessness; without law; a law-less attitude
17. "revealed" — ἀποκάλυψις (*apokalupsis*): to uncover, reveal, or unveil; something that has been veiled or hidden, but suddenly it becomes clear and visible to see; a sudden revealing; when the veil is removed,

what was hidden comes into plain view; what is behind the veil is no longer concealed or hidden from private or public view

18. "perdition" — ἀπώλεια (*apoleia*): doomed, rotten, ruinous, or decaying

SYNOPSIS

Paul's second letter to the believers in Thessalonica — what we've come to know as the book of Second Thessalonians — was written approximately 51 to 52 A.D., shortly after his first letter. As we saw in our previous lesson, Paul wrote these epistles to set the record straight regarding the rapture of the Church.

The believers in Thessalonica were new in the faith and not strongly rooted in the truth of Scripture. And in this vulnerable state, it seems that someone notable falsely informed them that the rapture had already taken place, and they had missed it. Thinking they were now Tribulation saints, the Thessalonians believers became fearful. To quell their fears, Paul wrote and said: "Now we beseech you, brethren, by the coming of our Lord Jesus Christ, and by our gathering together unto him, that ye be not soon shaken in mind, or be troubled, neither by spirit, nor by word, nor by letter as from us, as that the day of Christ is at hand" (2 Thessalonians 2:1,2).

The emphasis of this lesson:

Before Christ returns to rapture the Church, a great falling away will take place. To avoid being a part of this apostasy and mutinous rebellion against God, we must make every effort to guard ourselves from being deceived by delusional, distorted doctrine.

A SUMMARY OF SECOND THESSALONIANS 2:1,2
The Meaning of 'the Coming of Our Lord'

As we noted in our previous lesson, the word "beseech" in Second Thessalonians 2:1 is the Greek word *erotao*, and it describes *an earnest request by someone with a preferred position who gives a command he expects to be heard, honored, and obeyed*. Basically, Paul was stepping in and exercising his authority. He was the one who started the church in Thessalonica, and now from his preferred position, he was making a request that he expected them to hear and obey.

He said, "Now we beseech you, brethren, by the coming of our Lord Jesus Christ…" (2 Thessalonians 2:1). We saw that the word "coming" is the Greek word *parousia*, which technically, describes the second coming of Christ at the end of the seven-year tribulation. However, Paul used this word interchangeably from time to time to describe both the Second Coming of Christ and the Rapture of the Church. Therefore, in order to know how the word *parousia* is being used, we always need to translate it in the context of the surrounding verses and chapter.

In this case, we know for certain that Paul was not talking about the second coming of Christ at the end of the Tribulation because of the words he included at the end of the verse. Immediately after mentioning the coming of the Lord — the *parousia* — Paul clarified which event it was by saying "our gathering together unto Him." The phrase "gathering together" is the Greek word *episunagoge*, which depicts *that particular moment in the future when Jesus will gather His people to Himself at the end of the age.* This is the rapture of the Church.

There is one more interesting note about the word *parousia*, and that is it indicates a strong presence of God will be felt by true believers just before Jesus returns to gather the Church to Himself. That is, there will be a heightened awareness of God's presence alerting us to the fact that the rapture is imminent. Like metal is attracted to a magnet, the Holy Spirit living in us will feel a strong attraction or pull toward Jesus as He begins to descend into the lower atmosphere. This will alert us to the fact that the rapture is about to take place. Jesus never takes His people by surprise. The Bible confirms this saying, "Surely the Lord God does nothing, unless He reveals His secret to His servants…" (Amos 3:7 *NKJV*).

Yes, the Bible does say that Christ will come like "a thief in the night" (*see* 1 Thessalonians 5:2). But His coming will be like a thief for those who are living in darkness. As believers, we are children of the light, and as such, Christ's coming will not catch us by surprise (*see* 1 Thessalonians 5:4-6).

Putting the meanings of these words together, here is the *Renner Interpretive Version (RIV)* of Second Thessalonians 2:1:

> **Brothers, listen carefully, for I am asking you in the strongest of terms to hear what I am about to say and to do exactly what I'm asking you to do. The appearance of the Lord Jesus Christ is very near. The moment we have all longed and waited for is**

almost upon us! I'm talking about that moment when Jesus will finally gather us together for Himself.

Don't Be Shaken or Troubled By What You See and Hear

In Second Thessalonians 2:2, Paul went on to say, "…Be not soon shaken in mind, or be troubled, neither by spirit, nor by word, nor by letter as from us, as that the day of Christ is at hand." The word "soon" here is the Greek word *tacheos*, and it means *to do something as swiftly as possible*. Thus, the first part of this verse could be translated, "Don't be quickly or swiftly shaken."

This brings us to the word "shaken," which in Greek is the word *saleuo*, and it means *to shake; to waver, to totter; or to be moved*. To more fully understand this word's meaning, we must understand its tense. Here it points to events that cause shock or alarm; it refers to an event or repeated events so unexpected that it results in shock or distress. The word *saleuo* — translated here as "shaken" — can also signify *worry and inward anxiety* resulting from outward events that keep occurring repeatedly, as if there is no pause between shocking, debilitating, and nerve-racking happenings. One scholar translates it as *jumpiness* or *nervousness*.

Does this describe how you or those you know have been feeling? Are you jumpy, anxious, worried, or overwhelmed by the ongoing sequence of perplexing events that have been occurring? Indeed, it seems as though our society and the world itself is in a free fall. Jesus said that is what we can expect to happen at the very end of the age. In Matthew 24:8, He described the condition of the world as a pregnant woman who enters into labor. Just before delivering her child, her painful contractions get closer and closer and become harder and more intense until they are virtually on top of one another. In the same way, just before God's children are delivered from this world, the world will experience painful contractions that will become closer and closer and more intense right up until the time of the rapture of the Church. This is a clear sign that the Church age is ending and the seven-year tribulation is about to begin. Positioned between these two eras will be the rapture of the Church.

So Paul told the Thessalonian believers — and us — not to be soon shaken in mind or be troubled. The Greek word for "mind" here is the word *nous*, and it describes *the mind, will, and emotions*. Paul is saying,

"Get a grip on your thinking, and don't be troubled." The word "troubled" is the Greek word *throeo*, and it denotes *an inward fright that causes one to be filled with worry, anxiety, or fear*. Again, the tense of this word points to *an ongoing state of worry and inward anxiety* resulting from outward events that keep occurring repeatedly, as if there is no pause between these shocking, debilitating, and nerve-racking happenings.

Reject Rumors and Spiritual Revelations That Are Out of Sync With Scripture

To this, Paul added, "…Neither by spirit, nor by word…" (2 Thessalonians 2:2). We learned that the words "by spirit" refer to *a spiritual experience or spiritual utterance that is out of sync with the revealed Word of God*. Some translate this as *ecstatic utterances*. Here, it refers to *strange utterances, weird revelations, or euphoric proclamations that have no root in sound doctrine* and eventually produce the negative effect of spiritually upsetting the Church.

What Paul described in this verse is what we see happening now. There are some individuals who are teaching prophecy in such a way it is scaring people. Through Paul, the Holy Spirit is instructing us to turn a deaf ear to bizarre revelations that are not founded in God's Word. He also said not to be shaken or troubled "by word," which is a translation of the Greek phrase *dia logou*, and it means *by rumor*, nor by "letter," depicting *letters written with wrong motives*.

More than likely, you've heard people say things like, "Have you heard what so-and-so said?" "Did you see the latest video posted about the mark of the beast?" "Did you hear about where they believe this disease came from?" The fact is, there are so many conspiracy theories roaming around, it is hard to keep track of them all. If you believe everything you hear and see on the Internet or from news outlets, you'll soon become riddled with panic and terror. Instead, keep your eyes on Jesus and your ears open to what the Holy Spirit is saying. Dig deep into His Word and know what it says about the times in which we are living.

Putting the meanings of these words together, here is the *Renner Interpretive Version (RIV)* of Second Thessalonians 2:2:

> **Some things will be happening right before His coming that could shake you up quite a bit. I'm referring to events that will be so dramatic that they could leave your head spinning**

— occurrences of such a serious nature that many people will end up feeling alarmed, panicked, intimidated, and unnerved. Naturally speaking, these events could put your nerves on edge and make you feel apprehensive and insecure. How I wish I could tell you these incidents were going to be just a one-shot deal, but when they finally get rolling, they're going to keep coming and coming, one after another. That's why you have to determine not to be shaken or moved by anything you see or hear. You need to get a grip on your mind and refuse to allow yourselves to be traumatized by these events. If you let these things get to you, it won't be too long until you're a nervous wreck! That's why you have to decide beforehand that you are not going to give in and allow fright to penetrate its way into your mind and emotions until it runs your whole life. I also want to tell you not to be too surprised if people start making weird spiritual proclamations and off-the-wall utterances during the time just before the Lord comes. All kinds of strange things are going to happen during those days! It's going to get so bizarre that you might even receive a letter from some person who claims that the day of the Lord has already come! Who knows — he might even attach our name to it, alleging to have our endorsement. Or he might even send it as if it were written and sent from us.

That is the essence of what Paul said to the First-Century believers in Thessalonica. How fitting and relevant his words are to us living in these last of the last days.

Let No One Deceive You by Any Means

In Second Thessalonians 2:3, Paul added some very important information regarding the timing of the rapture. He said, "Let no man deceive you by any means: for that day shall not come, except there come a falling away first, and that man of sin be revealed, the son of perdition." This verse is packed with revelation, so let's take a look at some of the meanings of the key words and phrases it contains.

First, notice the phrase "no man." In Greek, it is the word *me tis*, and it denotes *a strong prohibition, sternly and strongly ordering the reader to reject some type of activity*. It is as if Paul was saying, "Let no man — absolutely no one whatsoever — deceive you by any means."

The Greek word for "deceive" here is not *planao* as it is in so many other places in Scripture. In this verse, it is the word *exapatao*, which means *cheat; seduce; or take advantage of by trickery*. Moreover, it means *to deceive by giving distorted impressions; to lure one into deception; using any means to promote delusional thinking and believing*. The individuals Paul was referring to here may be sincere in their desire to teach end-time prophecy, but they don't have the solid, biblical foundation from which to teach. Consequently, they are deluded and end up teaching distorted, delusional information that deceives people and steals their joy and peace.

Paul strongly and sternly warned not to let anyone like this lead us astray. To add emphasis, he included the phrase "by any means," which in Greek means *in no way at all; in no fashion* and it instructs us *"don't give them an inch."* In other words, we are to refuse to let anyone dominate us with their manipulations — especially in regard to "that day."

A 'Falling Away' Must Come Before the Rapture

What "day" was Paul referring to? It is the same day he mentioned in verses 1 and 2 — the day Jesus will gather all believers to Himself. It is the day of the rapture of the Church. Paul said before the rapture takes place and the Man of Sin is revealed, there must *first* come a falling away. The word "first" is the Greek word *proton*, which means *first in order; in first place*; or *to begin with*. The *first* in the sequence of events that must occur before the rapture is a *falling away*.

The words "falling away" are extremely important. In Greek, it is word *apostasia* and it always describes *a falling away or revolt; a political revolt or a mutiny*. It can also be translated as *a mutinous attitude of rebellion* or a general turning away from God. Unfortunately, there have been some who have erroneously declared that this "falling away" is the rapture of the Church, but that is a wrong interpretation. This apostasy is going to take place not only in the Church, but also in the world. Hence, we could say the rapture of the Church will not take place until a worldwide rebellion against God comes first.

If we were to go back in time about 50 years ago, we would find a very different world than the one in which we now live. If the Antichrist had tried to be introduced at that time, it wouldn't have worked, because the world would have recognized him. Back then, society was more Bible-based, and the people's general knowledge of Scripture would have exposed him. But as time has passed, people's knowledge of the Word has diminished, and the secret plan of the Antichrist has been in operation preparing the world for his arrival.

The fact is, there is a mutinous, rebellious attitude toward God permeating the world today, and it is growing. We are eye-witnesses to the *apostasia* — or falling away — Paul prophesied would take place in the last of the last days. By and large, the world has said, "We're not going to live with the old, outdated morals anymore. Nor are we going to live like the old fuddy-duddies of the past. We're going to frame a new world order with new morals and progressive standards. It's time we embrace a new way of thinking." These are the prime conditions needed for the Antichrist to come on the scene. A lawless world will willingly embrace a lawless leader.

The Antichrist Is the Man of 'Lawlessness'

Once the falling away has fully manifested, the Bible says, "…That man of sin [will] be revealed, the son of perdition" (2 Thessalonians 2:3). The word for "sin" in this verse is not *harmartia*, which is normally the word you would find in Scripture for "sin." Here, "sin" is the Greek word *anomia*, which is taken from the word *nomos*, the word for *law*. When an "*a*" is attached to the front, it means *to shuck off laws or standards; to throw off old trends, old traditions, old ways, or old modes*. Thus, the word *anomia* describes *lawlessness*; *without law*; or *a law-less attitude*.

So the man of "sin" is actually the Man of *Lawlessness*, and he will be "revealed" sooner than we think. This word "revealed" is the Greek word *apokalupsis*, which means *to uncover, reveal, or unveil*. It speaks of *something that has been veiled or hidden, but suddenly it becomes clear and visible to see*. It can also be translated as *a sudden revealing*. When the veil is removed, what was hidden comes into plain view; what is behind the veil is no longer concealed or hidden from private or public view.

Right now the Man of Sin, or the Man of Lawlessness, is hidden. His identity and whereabouts are concealed. But the day is coming when he will be unveiled for all to see. The apostle Paul also refers to him as "the son of perdition" (2 Thessalonians 2:3). The word "perdition" is the Greek word *apoleia*, and it describes something that is *doomed, rotten, ruinous, or decaying*. It is from the exact same Greek word used to describe *rotten meat that is filled with maggots*. The stench is so terrible it would take one's breath away.

This is how the Bible depicts the Antichrist — the Man of Lawlessness who will portray himself as the leader of the New World Order. Yet everything he touches is ultimately doomed to decay. Spiritually speaking, he is filled with rottenness like maggot-infested meat.

Putting the meanings of these words together, here is the *Renner Interpretive Version (RIV)* of Second Thessalonians 2:3:

> **In light of these things, I urge you to refuse to allow anyone to take advantage of you. For example, you won't need a letter to tell you when the day of the Lord has come. You ought to know by now that this day can't come until first a worldwide insurgency, rebellion, riot, and mutiny against God has come about in society. Once that occurs, the world will be primed, prepared, and ready to embrace the Man of Lawlessness, the one who hates law and has rebellion running in his blood. This is the long-awaited and predicted Son of Doom and Destruction, the one who brings rot and ruin to everything he touches. When the time is just right, he will finally come out of hiding and go public.**

What will happen once the Antichrist is revealed to the public? And who or what is stopping him from taking center stage right now? That will be our focus in Lesson 5.

STUDY QUESTIONS

> Study to shew thyself approved unto God, a workman that needeth not to be ashamed, rightly dividing the word of truth.
> — 2 Timothy 2:15

1. Carefully read Philippians 4:5; Hebrews 10:37; James 5:8; and Revelation 3:11 and 22:20. What recurring theme do all these verses have in common? What does this say to you personally?
2. Jesus said just before He returns to deliver God's children from this world, the world will experience painful contractions like a woman in labor (*see* Matthew 24:8). Unnerving and debilitating events will occur closer and closer together and become more intense right up until the time of the rapture. What connections can you draw between this truth and what Paul said in Romans 8:19-23?

3. What new insights did you learn about the "Man of Sin" — also known as the "Son of Perdition"?

PRACTICAL APPLICATION

> But be ye doers of the word, and not hearers only, deceiving your own selves.
> —James 1:22

1. Taking what you've learned so far in these first four lessons, name three important things about the rapture of the Church that you would share with close friends to encourage them in their faith.
2. Are you jumpy, anxious, worried, or overwhelmed by the ongoing sequence of perplexing events that have been occurring? What seems to be upsetting and frightening you most? How is this lesson helping you to see things from a better perspective?
3. In Isaiah's day, just as in ours, many people were getting caught up in listening to and looking for the latest conspiracy theories — including Isaiah (*see* Isaiah 8:11,12). But the Lord spoke to him and told him not to be afraid of what everyone else feared. Instead, God said:

> "The Lord of hosts — regard Him as holy and honor His holy name [by regarding Him as your only hope of safety], and let Him be your fear and let Him be your dread [lest you offend Him by your fear of man and distrust of Him]. And He shall be a sanctuary [a sacred and indestructible asylum to those who reverently fear and trust in Him]...."
> Isaiah 8:13,14 (*AMPC*)

Given the uncertain times in which we live, what is God speaking to you in this passage?

LESSON 5

TOPIC
The Coming of the Antichrist

SCRIPTURES
1. **2 Thessalonians 2:3-6** — Let no man deceive you by any means: for that day shall not come, except there come a falling away first, and that man of sin be revealed, the son of perdition; Who opposeth and exalteth himself above all that is called God, or that is worshipped; so that he as God sitteth in the temple of God, shewing himself that he is God. Remember ye not, that, when I was yet with you, I told you these things? And now ye know what withholdeth that he might be revealed in his time.

GREEK WORDS
1. "no man" — **μή τις** (*me tis*): denotes a strong prohibition, sternly and strongly ordering the reader to reject some type of activity
2. "deceive" — **ἐξαπατάω** (*exapatao*): cheat; seduce; to take advantage of by trickery; to deceive by giving distorted impressions; to lure one into deception; using any means to promote delusional thinking and believing
3. "by any means" — **κατὰ μηδένα τρόπον** (*kata medena tropon*): in no way at all; in no fashion; "don't give them an inch"; refuse to let them dominate you with their manipulations
4. "falling away" — **ἀποστασία** (*apostasia*): a falling away or revolt; describes political revolt; a mutiny
5. "first" — **πρῶτον** (*proton*): first in order; in first place; to begin with
6. "sin" — **ἀνομία** (*anomia*): lawlessness; without law; a lawless attitude
7. "revealed" — **ἀποκάλυψις** (*apokalupsis*): to uncover, reveal, or unveil; something that has been veiled or hidden, but suddenly it becomes clear and visible to see; a sudden revealing; when the veil is removed, what was hidden comes into plain view; what is behind the veil is no longer concealed or hidden from private or public view
8. "perdition" — **ἀπώλεια** (*apoleia*): doomed, rotten, ruinous, or decaying

9. "opposeth" — ἀντίκειμαι (*antikeimai*): opposed to or against everything that is established; a clear reference to the Antichrist
10. "exalteth" — ὑπεραίρω (*huperairo*): to exalt oneself; to exceedingly exalt oneself; to be exalted highly; the idea of one being too highly exalted
11. "above" — ἐπί (*epi*): above; over; implies a position of superiority
12. "all" — πάντα (*panta*): all, nothing excluded
13. "called" — λεγόμενον (*legomenon*): so-called; being called; referred to as
14. "God" — Θεός (*Theos*): proper name for God
15. "worshipped" — σέβασμα (*sebasma*): divine; anything that can be worshiped and includes the worship of God
16. "sitteth" — καθίζω (*kathidzo*): to sit down; to be seated
17. "temple" — ναός (*naos*): a temple or a highly decorated shrine; the image of vaulted ceilings, marble, granite, gold, silver, and highly decorated ornamentation; the most sacred, innermost part of a temple; the holy of holies
18. "shewing" — ἀποδείκνυμι (*apodeiknumi*): refers to something outwardly observable or done visibly to authenticate, prove, or guarantee a claim to onlookers; to make a vivid presentation; to demonstrate
19. "now" — νῦν (*nun*): now, at this very moment in time
20. "withholdeth" — κατέχω (*katecho*): to hold fast; to hold down; to hold back; to suppress; to restrain; to hinder
21. "in his time" — ἐν τῷ ἑαυτοῦ καιρῷ (*en to heautou kairo*): a specific season or an opportunity

SYNOPSIS

The New Testament clearly tells us that at some point in the future, an evil ruler is going to arise on the world scene and take total control of the world system for a brief amount of time. The apostle Paul calls this mutinous monarch the Antichrist and says that before he is revealed, some specific things need to take place. In Second Thessalonians 2:3, he said:

> **"Let no man deceive you by any means: for that day shall not come, except there come a falling away first, and that man of sin be revealed, the son of perdition."**

We have seen that this "falling away" Paul spoke of will occur just before the rapture of the Church. Once Christ gathers His people together, the

"Son of Perdition" will be revealed. Let's briefly review the key words and phrases in verse 3 and then take a closer look at what the Antichrist will do once he has gone public.

The emphasis of this lesson:

The Antichrist is the Son of Perdition who is destined to bring doom and destruction to all the earth. Once the supernatural restrainer is removed and the Lawless One's identity is revealed, he will seek to exalt himself above God and take a permanent seat in God's temple.

A REVIEW OF SECOND THESSALONIANS 2:3

"No man" in Greek is the word *me tis*. It denotes *a strong prohibition, sternly and strongly ordering the reader to reject some type of activity*. In this case, Paul strongly warned, "Let no man — absolutely no one whatsoever — deceive you by any means."

"Deceive" is the Greek word *exapatao*, which means *to cheat; seduce; or to take advantage of by trickery; to deceive by giving distorted impressions; to lure one into deception; using any means to promote delusional thinking and believing*. The Thessalonian believers were listening to teachers who were trying to teach prophecy but who didn't have a solid, biblical foundation. Consequently, they were teaching distorted, delusional information. They actually told the Thessalonians that the Rapture had come, and they had missed it.

"By any means" in Greek means *in no way at all; in no fashion* and it instructs us *"don't give them an inch."* Paul added these words to emphasize his stern prohibition. In other words, we are to refuse to let anyone dominate us with his or her manipulations — especially in regard to "that day."

"That day" refers to the same day Paul mentioned in verses 1 and 2. It is the rapture of the Church — the day Jesus will come and gather all believers to Himself. Prophetically, Paul pointed from the First Century, where he was, all the way to the very end of the age, just before the Antichrist would be revealed, and he said there would be a falling away.

"Falling away" is the Greek word *apostasia*, and it always describes *a falling away, a revolt, or a mutiny*. Plutarch used this same word to describe *a political revolt*. It can also be translated as *a mutinous attitude of rebellion* or a general *turning away from God*. The word *apostasia* also occurs in the Septuagint version of Joshua 22:22, where it conveys the idea of *rebellion against God*. It is an attitude that says, "*We don't need You anymore, and we're not going to follow You.*" This attitude will be widespread in the Church and the world just before Christ returns. Indeed, we see it all around us today.

"**First.**" Writing under the inspiration of the Holy Spirit, Paul said that this falling away must happen "first." In Greek, this is the word *proton*, which means *first in order*; *in first place*; or *to begin with*. The *first* in the sequence of events that must occur before the rapture is a *falling away*. A worldwide, mutinous rebellion against God has to happen first in order to prepare society to willingly embrace the Antichrist.

If we were to go back in time 50 years, we would find that the world was a very different place. Back then, society was more Bible-based, and because of the people's general knowledge of Scripture, they would have recognized and rejected the Antichrist. But as time has passed, people's knowledge of the Word has diminished, and the world has become a lawless place. The spirit of antichrist has been at work since the days of the Early Church (*see* 1 John 4:3), secretly preparing the world for his eventual arrival. Today, we have an entire generation that doesn't know the Bible and has thrown off the past standards and morals we once lived by. Like the Old Testament days of the judges, everyone is doing what seems right in his or her own eyes (*see* Judges 21:25). Our lawless world is primed and prepared to receive a lawless leader.

"**Man of Sin**" is one of the names the Bible gives for the Antichrist. Once the falling away has fully manifested, the Bible says, "…That man of sin [will] be revealed, the son of perdition" (2 Thessalonians 2:3). The word for "sin" here is the Greek word *anomia*, which is taken from the word *nomos*, meaning *law*. When an "*a*" is attached to its front, it means *lawlessness*; *without law*; or *a law-less attitude*. Thus, the man of "sin" is the Man of *Lawlessness*. He will probably claim to be a progressive thinker, advocating a new, more contemporary way of living. But in reality, he will lead the people of the world into a lawless society that is free from God's commandments — absent of His peace, protection, and goodness.

"**Revealed**" is the Greek word *apokalupsis*, which is a compound of the word *apo*, meaning *away*, and the word *kalupsis*, which describes *something that is veiled, covered, concealed, or hidden*. When these two words are compounded to form the word *apokalupsis*, it depicts *the pulling back of a* *curtain or veil, exposing something that was formerly concealed or hidden from view.* In this case, when the curtain is pulled back, the Antichrist — who will have been there all along — will appear center-stage on the world scene, claiming to have the answers to the world's needs.

"**Son of Perdition**" is another name given to the Antichrist by the apostle Paul in Second Thessalonians 2:3. The word "perdition" is the Greek word *apoleia*, and it describes something that is *doomed, rotten, ruinous, or decaying*. It is the same Greek word used to describe *rotten meat that is filled with maggots*. This is the word the Holy Spirit prompted Paul to use to describe the Antichrist. Although he will boast of leading the world to a higher and better day, he will bring it to a place of total *decay* and *destruction*.

Putting the meanings of these words together, here is the *Renner Interpretive Version (RIV)* of Second Thessalonians 2:3:

> **In light of these things, I urge you to refuse to allow anyone to take advantage of you. For example, you won't need a letter to tell you when the day of the Lord has come. You ought to know by now that this day can't come until first a worldwide insurgency, rebellion, riot, and mutiny against God has come about in society. Once that occurs, the world will be primed, prepared, and ready to embrace the Man of Lawlessness, the one who hates law and has rebellion running in his blood. This is the long-awaited and predicted Son of Doom and Destruction, the one who brings rot and ruin to everything he touches. When the time is just right, he will finally come out of hiding and go public.**

The Antichrist Will Exalt Himself 'Above All That Is Called God'

Once the Church has been raptured and the Antichrist has been revealed, the Man of Lawlessness will swiftly move in to action. Paul tells us more about him in Second Thessalonians 2:4:

> "**Who opposeth and exalteth himself above all that is called God, or that is worshipped; so that he as God sitteth in the temple of God, shewing himself that he is God.**

Notice that the Antichrist "opposeth…all that is called God, or that is worshipped…." The Greek word for "opposeth" is *antikeimai*, which means *opposed to* or *against everything that is established*. This is a clear reference to the Antichrist. The name "Antichrist" means *against Christ*. Clearly, he is against anything that resembles Christ and His established ways of righteousness in His Word.

Along with opposing everything of God, the Antichrist will "…exalteth himself above all that is called God…." The word "exalteth" is the Greek word *huperairo*, and it means *to exalt oneself; to exceedingly exalt oneself; to be exalted highly*. It is *the idea of one being too highly exalted*. The Antichrist will exceedingly exalt himself "above all that is called God."

The word "above" in Greek is *epi*, which means *above* or *over*, and implies *a position of superiority and domination*. The word "all" is *panta* in Greek, which means *all, nothing excluded*. And the word "worshipped" is the Greek word *sebasma*, which describes *anything that can be worshiped, including the worship of God*. The fact that the Antichrist will exalt himself as superior to all that is called God or that is worshiped means he will elevate himself above all forms of religion in the world, not just Christianity. He will subdue and crush all that is worshiped and esteemed as divine.

He Will Seat Himself In the Temple of God

Paul went on to say the Antichrist will present himself as God and will "…sitteth in the temple of God…" (2 Thessalonians 2:4). The word "sitteth" is the Greek word *kathidzo*, which means *to sit down* or *to be seated*, and it carries the idea of being *permanently seated*. The Antichrist will attempt to permanently seat himself in the "temple of God." The Greek word for "temple" here is *naos*, which describes *a temple* or *a highly decorated shrine*. It depicts *the image of vaulted ceilings, marble, granite, gold, silver, and highly decorated ornamentation*.

What's interesting is the word *naos* is the exact same word used in the Septuagint version of the Old Testament to describe *the Holy of Holies — the most sacred, innermost part of a temple*. Because this word was used, many scholars believe it is a reference to a future, rebuilt temple in Jerusalem where the Antichrist will enter and attempt to set himself up as God incarnate.

He Will Demonstrate Lying Signs and Wonders

Moreover, the Bible says he will be "...shewing himself that he is God" (2 Thessalonians 2:4). The word "shewing" in Greek is *apodeiknumi*, and it refers to *something outwardly observable or done visibly to authenticate, prove, or guarantee a claim to onlookers*. It means *to make a vivid presentation* or to demonstrate something. This is the same word used throughout the New Testament to describe the signs and wonders the apostles did that proved the authenticity of the Gospel.

There is really nothing original about Satan. He cannot create anything. He can only corrupt or make a counterfeit of what God has created. Like Satan, the Antichrist will act as a copycat and bring forth supernatural activity to deceive people into believing that he is God, and many will swallow it hook, line, and sinker.

Putting the meanings of these words together, here is the *Renner Interpretive Version (RIV)* of Second Thessalonians 2:4:

> **Do you understand who I am talking about? I'm describing that person who will be so against God and everything connected with the worship of God that, if you can imagine it, he will even try to put himself on a pedestal above God Himself — sitting in God's rightful place in the temple and publicly proclaiming himself to be God!**

The Great Restrainer

In Second Thessalonians 2:5, the apostle Paul asked the believers, "Remember ye not, that, when I was yet with you, I told you these things?" Then in verse 6, he began to remind them of what he told them. "And now ye know what withholdeth that he might be revealed in his time." So something has been holding back Satan from introducing the Antichrist to the world. The question is, who or what is it?

The word "now" is the Greek word *nun*, which means *now, at this very moment in time*. Basically Paul said, "In this very moment, you should already know what withholdeth the Antichrist." The word "withholdeth" in Greek is *katecho*, and it means *to hold fast; to hold down; to hold back; to suppress; to restrain*, or *to hinder*. What is this force that is restraining, suppressing, and holding back the floodgates of evil from pouring into the world and taking it over?

When Paul wrote this letter to the believers in Thessalonica during the First Century, they believed the restrainer was one of five possibilities.

The Roman Senate was one potential candidate. The Early Church believed that if the Roman Senate wasn't in power, Nero would have totally unleashed evil throughout the entire Roman Empire. But since the Roman Senate has come and gone and the Antichrist hasn't been revealed, it can't be the restrainer.

God Almighty Himself has also been viewed as the one who "withholdeth," and **the Holy Spirit** is a third option people have gravitated toward. However, because the Holy Spirit is always going to be on the earth — and scripture says the restrainer will be taken out of the way (2 Thessalonians 2:7) — He cannot be the great restrainer.

The Church is possibly number four, and **Michael the archangel** is number five. The reason Michael has been considered the great restrainer is because Scripture speaks in several places of how he stood against Satan. In the book of Daniel, we see Michael holding back evil forces, and in the book of Jude, he stood against Satan who was arguing with him over the body of Moses (*see* Jude 1:9).

Of these five possibilities, one is confirmed in the context of Scripture as being the great restrainer who is holding back the coming of the Antichrist. **It is the Church.** As long as the Church is on the earth, it is holding back the onslaught of evil. Imagine what would happen if God's people were abruptly removed — let's say in the twinkling of an eye. That's the rapture! In a moment — an *atomos* of time — the dead in Christ will be raised to life, and the believers who are alive on the earth will be instantaneously caught up into the air. When the Church is evacuated from the earth, the restrainer will be removed and the Antichrist will be revealed.

Paul said, "Now ye know what withholdeth that he might be revealed in his time" (2 Thessalonians 2:6). The word "revealed" is once again the Greek word *apokalupsis*, which depicts *the pulling back of a curtain or veil, exposing something that was formerly concealed, veiled, or hidden from view*. When the Church — which is full of the Holy Spirit and God's presence and power — is raptured from the earth, the Antichrist will be revealed, and it will take place "in his time." This phrase is from the root word *kairos*, which refers to *a specific season* or *an opportunity*. At the appointed time, when conditions are most favorable, the Antichrist will arise and seize the opportunity to unleash the full force of evil in the world.

Putting the meanings of these words together, here is the *Renner Interpretive Version (RIV)* of Second Thessalonians 2:6:

> **Now in light of everything I've told you before, you ought to be well aware by now that there is a supernatural force at work that is preventing the materialization of this person and the disclosure of his identity. This restraining force I'm referring to is so strong that it is currently putting on the brakes and holding back the unveiling of this wicked person, stalling and postponing his manifestation. But when the right moment comes, this evil one will no longer be withheld, and he will emerge on the world scene! The screen that has been hiding his true identity and guarding him from world view will suddenly be pulled back and evaporate — and he will step out on center stage to let everyone know who he is.**

So if anyone tries to tell you that the Antichrist is going to show up at any moment, you can know with certainty that he will not be revealed until the Church is out of here. We are the great restrainer!

STUDY QUESTIONS

> Study to shew thyself approved unto God, a workman that needeth
> not to be ashamed, rightly dividing the word of truth.
> — 2 Timothy 2:15

1. The Bible says the Antichrist will enter the temple of God and attempt to set himself up as God and receive the worship and praise that is due God. Who does this remind you of in Scripture, and what happened to him as a result? (See Isaiah 14:12-16.)

2. Did you know that the Antichrist is going to "oppose and exalt himself above all that is called God or that is worshiped" (*see* 2 Thessalonians 2:4)? How does the meaning of the words in this verse open your eyes to things you never saw before about the Antichrist and the condition of the world during the Tribulation?

PRACTICAL APPLICATION

> But be ye doers of the word, and not hearers only,
> deceiving your own selves.
> —James 1:22

1. More than likely, you have unsaved family members and friends who need to receive Christ before Jesus raptures the Church and the Antichrist unleashes his sinister schemes on the earth. Take the time right now to write down the names of your loved ones and begin to regularly and passionately pray for them.
2. Can you remember who prayed for you to be saved? Have you ever taken the time to thank that person and express your gratefulness for his or her investment of time and energy in your salvation? Why not do so today by making a phone call or sending a personal note.
3. According to First Timothy 2:4, God wants "…all men to be saved, and to come unto the knowledge of the truth." This includes your family members and friends. In addition to praying for their salvation, pray and ask the Holy Spirit to give you an opportunity to share the message of the Gospel with them. If you feel they're closed to you, pray for God to send people across their path that they admire and are open to who will share the truth with them.

LESSON 6

TOPIC

Who Hinders These Developments Now?

SCRIPTURES

1. **2 Thessalonians 2:3-8** — Let no man deceive you by any means: for that day shall not come, except there come a falling away first, and that man of sin be revealed, the son of perdition; Who opposeth and exalteth himself above all that is called God, or that is worshipped; so that he as God sitteth in the temple of God, shewing himself that he is God. Remember ye not, that, when I was yet with you, I told you

these things? And now ye know what withholdeth that he might be revealed in his time. For the mystery of iniquity doth already work: only he who now letteth will let, until he be taken out of the way. And then shall that Wicked be revealed....

GREEK WORDS

1. "no man" — μή τις (*me tis*): denotes a strong prohibition, sternly and strongly ordering the reader to reject some type of activity
2. "deceive" — ἐξαπατάω (*exapatao*): cheat; seduce; to take advantage of by trickery; to deceive by giving distorted impressions; to lure one into deception; using any means to promote delusional thinking and believing
3. "by any means" — κατὰ μηδένα τρόπον (*kata medena tropon*): in no way at all; in no fashion; "don't give them an inch"; refuse to let them dominate you with their manipulations
4. "falling away" — ἀποστασία (*apostasia*): a falling away or revolt; describes political revolt; a mutiny
5. "first" — πρῶτον (*proton*): first in order; in first place; first in order; to begin with
6. "sin" — ἀνομία (*anomia*): lawlessness; without law; a lawless attitude
7. "revealed" — ἀποκάλυψις (*apokalupsis*): to uncover, reveal, or unveil; something that has been veiled or hidden, but suddenly it becomes clear and visible to see; a sudden revealing; when the veil is removed, what was hidden comes into plain view; what is behind the veil is no longer concealed or hidden from private or public view
8. "perdition" — ἀπώλεια (*apoleia*): doomed, rotten, ruinous, or decaying
9. "opposeth" — ἀντίκειμαι (*antikeimai*): opposed to or against everything that is established
10. "exalteth" — ὑπεραίρω (*huperairo*): to exalt oneself; to exceedingly exalt oneself; to be exalted highly; the idea of one being too highly exalted
11. "above" — ἐπί (*epi*): above; over; implies a position of superiority
12. "all" — πάντα (*panta*): all, nothing excluded
13. "called" — λεγόμενον (*legomenon*): so-called; being called; referred to as
14. "God" — Θεός (*Theos*): proper name for God

15. "worshipped" — **σέβασμα** (*sebasma*): divine; anything that can be worshiped and includes the worship of God
16. "sitteth" — **καθίζω** (*kathidzo*): to sit down; to be seated
17. "temple" — **ναός** (*naos*): a temple or a highly decorated shrine; the image of vaulted ceilings, marble, granite, gold, silver, and highly decorated ornamentation; the most sacred, innermost part of a temple; the Holy of Holies
18. "shewing" — **ἀποδείκνυμι** (*apodeiknumi*): indisputably refers to something outwardly observable or done visibly to authenticate, prove, or guarantee a claim to onlookers; to prove by showing; to make a vivid presentation; to demonstrate
19. "now" — **νῦν** (*nun*): now, at this present moment, at this very moment in time
20. "withholdeth" — **κατέχω** (*katecho*): to hold fast; to hold down; to hold back; to suppress; to restrain; to hinder
21. "in his time" — **ἐν τῷ ἑαυτοῦ καιρῷ** (*en to heautou kairo*): denotes a specific season or an opportunity
22. "mystery" — **μυστήριον** (*musterion*): a mystery; secret; once hidden, but now revealed
23. "iniquity" — **ἀνομία** (*anomia*): lawlessness; without law; a lawless attitude
24. "already" — **ἤδη** (*ede*): no new development, but something that has been at work for quite some time
25. "work" — **ἐνεργέω** (*energeo*): energized to fulfillment; a force propelling something forward or an energy that ignites a process and facilitates it all the way to its conclusion
26. "only" — **μόνον** (*monon*): alone; only; no one else
27. "now" — **ἄρτι** (*arti*): now; just now; at this moment; in the immediate present
28. "letteth" — **κατέχω** (*katecho*): to hold fast; to hold down; to hold back; to suppress; to restrain; to hinder
29. "will let" — **κατέχω** (*katecho*): to hold fast; to hold down; to hold back; to suppress; to restrain; to hinder
30. "until" — **ἕως** (*heos*): until that moment
31. "be taken" — **γένηται** (*genetai*): from **γίνομαι** (*ginomai*), a surprising event

32. "out of the way" — ἐκ μέσου (*ek mesou*): out of the middle; out of the midst; out of the middle of things

SYNOPSIS

So far in our study, we have learned that the church in Thessalonica was started by the apostle Paul, and the believers there were young in the faith. It seems that they were listening to inaccurate prophecy teachers who told them that the rapture of the Church had already taken place and that they had been left behind. Thinking that they were living in the tribulation, these believers became greatly distressed. Paul wrote to them and set the record straight, informing them that the Rapture had *not* taken place yet. To this he added, "Let no man deceive you by any means: for that day shall not come, except there come a falling away first, and that man of sin be revealed, the son of perdition."

The emphasis of this lesson:

Satan and his minions have been busily working their secret plan of lawlessness since the founding days of the Church. There is only one thing that is holding back the Antichrist from being revealed and releasing the full force of evil on the earth — the Church.

A SUMMARY OF SECOND THESSALONIANS 2:3
Don't Be Deceived by Inaccurate Prophecy Teachers

When Paul said, "Let no man deceive you," the phrase "no man" in Greek is the word *me tis*. It is *an emphatic and strong order to the hearer not to let anyone whatsoever deceive you*. The word "deceive" is the Greek word *exapatao*, and it means *to cheat; seduce; or to take advantage of by trickery*. It carries *the idea of being deceived by giving distorted impressions; to lure one into deception; using any means to promote delusional thinking and believing*. These inaccurate teachers may have been very sincere in their desire to teach Bible prophecy, but they were sincerely wrong because they didn't have a solid grasp of Scripture.

Urgently, Paul warned, "Let no man deceive you by any means…" (2 Thessalonians 2:3). The phrase "by no means" in Greek means *in no way at all; in no fashion; "don't give them an inch."* This was the equivalent of Paul saying, "Don't give delusional teachers or delusional teaching an inch in your life. Know that what you are hearing is biblically sound information." In other words, we are to refuse to let anyone dominate us with their manipulations — especially in regards to "that day."

A 'Falling Away' Must Precede the 'Catching Away'

Paul continued in verse 3, "…For that day shall not come, except there come a falling away first…" "That day" speaks of the rapture of the Church — it's the same day Paul talked about in verses 1 and 2. The phrase "falling away" is the Greek word *apostasia*, and it always describes *a revolt, a mutiny, a political revolt,* or *a mutinous attitude of rebellion.* Generally speaking, the *apostasia* is *a turning away from God.* It is an attitude that says, "We don't need You anymore, God, and we're not going to follow You." This attitude has become prevalent not only in the world, but also in the Church and will continue to increase right up to the time of the rapture.

The environment of the world is going to become so mutinous and hostile to God in the last of the last days it will help trigger the return of Christ. We see this in Paul's description of the Rapture in First Thessalonians 4:17, which says, "Then we which are alive and remain shall be caught up together with them in the clouds…." The word for "caught up" is a form of the Greek word *harpadzó*, which means *to snatch out of imminent danger, just in the nick of time.* In other words, those who are spiritually vibrant and alive at the end of the age will very likely feel as though they are in extreme grave danger. But Jesus is going to descend from Heaven with a mighty shout, the voice of the archangel, and the last trump and rescue us from the wrath that is to come (*see* 1 Thessalonians 4:16).

The Bible states that after the falling away (a mutinous rebellion) and the catching away (the rapture of the Church), "…That man of sin [will] be revealed, the son of perdition" (2 Thessalonians 2:3). The word "sin" here is the Greek word *anomia*, which is taken from the word *nomos*, meaning *law.* When it is preceded by an *"a",* it means *lawlessness*; *without law*; or *a law-less attitude.* Although the Antichrist will likely claim to be a progressive thinker that will move the world forward in to a bold new future, he will actually be the Man of *Lawlessness*, the Son of *Perdition*.

The Greek word for "perdition" is *apoleia*, and it describes anything that is *doomed, rotten, ruinous, or decaying.* It is the same Greek word used to describe *rotten meat that is filled with maggots.* This is the word the Holy

Spirit prompted Paul to use to describe the Antichrist. Everything he touches will be doomed and turn to ruin.

Putting the meanings of these words together, here is the *Renner Interpretive Version (RIV)* of Second Thessalonians 2:3:

> In light of these things, I urge you to refuse to allow anyone to take advantage of you. For example, you won't need a letter to tell you when the day of the Lord has come. You ought to know by now that this day can't come until first a worldwide insurgency, rebellion, riot, and mutiny against God has come about in society. Once that occurs, the world will be primed, prepared, and ready to embrace the Man of Lawlessness, the one who hates law and has rebellion running in his blood. This is the long-awaited and predicted Son of Doom and Destruction, the one who brings rot and ruin to everything he touches. When the time is just right, he will finally come out of hiding and go public.

What Will The Antichrist Be Like When He Finally Goes Public?

After Jesus has returned and raptured the Church, the Antichrist will swiftly step out of the shadows and take center stage. This Man of Lawlessness, the Son of Perdition, will be the epitome of evil, achieving an intensity of blasphemy never displayed before by anyone on the earth. Second Thessalonians 2:4 says he will "…opposeth and exalteth himself above all that is called God, or that is worshipped; so that he as God sitteth in the temple of God, shewing himself that he is God."

The word "opposeth" in Greek is *antikeimai*, which means *opposed to* or *against everything that is established*. This tells us the Antichrist will be against every moral, every standard, and every previous societal norm that was once set in stone. The name "Antichrist" means *against Christ*. Clearly, he will be against anything that resembles Christ and His established ways of righteousness.

Along with opposing everything of God, he will "…exalteth himself above all that is called God…." The word "exalteth" is the Greek word *huperairo*, and it means *to exceedingly exalt oneself, to be exalted highly*. It carries *the idea of one being too highly exalted.* The Antichrist will exceedingly exalt himself "above all that is called God."

The word "above" is a translation of the Greek word *epi*, which implies *a position of superiority and domination.* The word "all" is the Greek word *panta*, which indicates *all, nothing excluded.* And the word "worshipped" is the Greek word *sebasma*, which denotes *anything that can be worshiped, including the worship of God.* Although the Antichrist will be particularly against Christianity, he will also be against all world religions and so-called gods, elevating himself as superior to all that is worshiped and esteemed as divine.

Paul went on to say the Antichrist will "…sitteth in the temple of God…" (2 Thessalonians 2:4), which means he will attempt *to permanently seat himself* in the "temple of God." The Greek word for "temple" here is *naos*, which describes *a temple* or *a highly decorated shrine.* It is the same Greek word used in the Septuagint version of the Old Testament to describe *the Holy of Holies — the most sacred, innermost part of a temple.* The use of the word *naos* suggests that the Antichrist is going to enter a third temple yet to be built in the city of Jerusalem and take his seat in the position that belongs solely to God, "…shewing himself that he is God" (2 Thessalonians 2:4).

In Greek, the word "shewing" is *apodeiknumi*, and it describes *something outwardly observable or done visibly to authenticate, prove, or guarantee a claim to onlookers.* It is the same word used throughout the New Testament to describe the signs and wonders the apostles did to make *a vivid presentation* that proved the authenticity of the Gospel. Thus, the Antichrist will conjure up supernatural manifestations as evidence that he is God in the flesh, and the people of the earth will be awestruck by it.

Putting the meanings of these words together, here is the *Renner Interpretive Version (RIV)* of Second Thessalonians 2:4:

> **Do you understand who I am talking about? I'm describing that person who will be so against God and everything connected with the worship of God that, if you can imagine it, he will even try to put himself on a pedestal above God Himself — sitting in God's rightful place in the temple and publicly proclaiming himself to be God!**

Who Is the Restrainer Preventing the Antichrist from Being Unmasked?

Next, the apostle Paul turned to the Thessalonian believers and asked, "Remember ye not, that, when I was yet with you, I told you these things?" (2 Thessalonians 2:5). Then in verse 6, he proceeded to say, "And now ye know what withholdeth that he might be revealed in his time."

The word "now" is the Greek word *nun*, which means *now, at this very moment in time*. A better translation of the first part of this verse would be, *"Now, since I have already told you all these things, you ought to already know...."* what withholdeth the Antichrist. In Greek, the word "withholdeth" is *katecho*, which means *to hold fast; to hold down; to hold back; to suppress; to restrain*, or *to hinder*. What is the supernatural force present in the world right now that is restraining, suppressing, and holding back the floodgates of evil from pouring in? What is stalling and postponing the manifestation of the Antichrist in this very moment? The answer to this question has been the subject of great theological debate for two thousand years and has produced five prime possibilities.

Possibility #1: The Roman Senate

Many in the Early Church believed Second Thessalonians 2:6 described *the Roman Senate* and that God was using the senate to hold back Nero from totally unleashing evil throughout the Roman Empire. But since the Roman Senate has come and gone and the Antichrist hasn't been revealed, they can't be the restrainer.

Possibility #2: God Almighty Himself

Some have believed the restrainer is *God Almighty Himself*.

Possibility #3: The Holy Spirit

Others have viewed that the one who "withholdeth" is *the Holy Spirit*. But the Holy Spirit will never be removed from the earth. He will be here even during the tribulation, working to bring about salvation in the lives of anyone whose heart is open to Him. Thus, the Holy Spirit cannot be the restrainer.

Possibility #4: The Church

There are also those who believe *the Church* is the supernatural restrainer on the earth.

Possibility #5: Michael the Archangel

The reason Michael has been considered the one holding back the Antichrist is because Scripture talks about how he stood against evil principalities in the book of Daniel, and in the book of Jude he stood against Satan who was arguing with him over the body of Moses (*see* Jude 1:9).

Out of these five possibilities, *the Church of the Lord Jesus Christ* is the one that best fits the description in Scripture as being the great restrainer. As long as the Church is on the earth, it is holding back the onslaught of evil. Once all of God's people are abruptly removed in the rapture, the Antichrist will "…be revealed in his time" (2 Thessalonians 2:6).

We saw that the word "revealed" is a translation of the Greek word *apokalupsis*. It is a compound of the word *apo*, meaning *away*, and the word *kalupsis*, which describes *something that is veiled, covered, concealed, or hidden*. When these two words come together to form the word *apokalupsis*, it depicts *the pulling back of a curtain or veil, exposing something that was formerly concealed or hidden from view*. When the Church is raptured from the earth, the Antichrist will be revealed, and it will take place "in his time." The word "time" here is the Greek word *kairos*, which signifies *a specific season* or *an opportunity*. The Antichrist is an opportunist. When the conditions in the world are just right, he will seize the opportunity and suddenly appear on the world's stage.

Putting the meanings of these words together, here is the *Renner Interpretive Version (RIV)* of Second Thessalonians 2:6:

> **Now in light of everything I've told you before, you ought to be well aware by now that there is a supernatural force at work that is preventing the materialization of this person and the disclosure of his identity. This restraining force I'm referring to is so strong that it is currently putting on the brakes and holding back the unveiling of this wicked person, stalling and postponing his manifestation. But when the right moment comes, this evil one will no longer be withheld, and he will emerge on the world scene! The screen that has been hiding his true identity and guarding him from world view will suddenly**

be pulled back and evaporate — and he will step out on center stage to let everyone know who he is.

The 'Mystery of Iniquity' Is Already at Work

In Second Thessalonians 2:7, the apostle Paul goes on to say, "For the mystery of iniquity doth already work: only he who now letteth will let, until he be taken out of the way." The word "mystery" is the Greek word *musterion*, and it describes *a mystery or secret; something once hidden, but now revealed*. This word carries the idea of a secret plan that has been hidden from the masses and only a select few are aware of it.

Paul said this is the mystery of "iniquity." In Greek, the word "iniquity" is *anomia* — the same word translated as "sin" in Second Thessalonians 2:3. It means *lawlessness; without law;* or *a lawless attitude*. The Bible says there is a hidden plan of lawlessness that is already at work. The word "already" is the Greek word *ede*, which indicates *something that is not a new development, but that has been at work for quite some time*. And the word "work" in verse 7 is a translation of the Greek word *energeo*, meaning *energized to fulfillment*. It describes *a force propelling something forward or an energy that ignites a process and facilitates it all the way to its conclusion*. This lets us know the devil has been working a long time to modify the world to get it ready for the Antichrist. He and his demonic forces have conspired together and have been stealthily working their plan since the days of the Early Church to prepare the world for the Man of Lawlessness.

What Is Stopping Satan from Fully Manifesting His Evil Scheme?

Looking again at Second Thessalonians 2:7, Paul said, "…Only he who now letteth will let, until he be taken out of the way." The word "only" is the Greek word *monon*, which means *alone; only; no one else*. And the word "now" is the Greek word *arti*, which means *now; just now; at this moment; in the immediate present*. The meaning of these two words explicitly tell us that there is *only one restraining force at this very moment* holding back the mystery of iniquity from being fully activated on the earth — only one thing that is stopping the Antichrist from being revealed and taking control of everything.

Notice the words "letteth" and "let." They are the same Greek word repeated twice — the word *katecho*, which means *to hold fast; to hold down;*

to hold back; to suppress; to restrain; to hinder. It is the exact same word that appears in verse 6 and is translated as "withholdeth." So from the First Century all the way to the end of the age, there has been and will be a supernatural restrainer holding back the forces of evil from fully taking control. Who has been on the earth since that time and will be through the end of the age? It is *the Church.* Jesus declared, "…I will build my church; and the gates of hell shall not prevail against it" (Matthew 16:18). This tells us how powerful the Church is. It is the restraining force in the earth.

Paul said that the Antichrist will remain hidden "…until he [the restrainer] be taken out of the way" (2 Thessalonians 2:7). The word "until" is the Greek word *heos*, and it means *until that precise moment.* The phrase "be taken" in Greek is *genetai*, which is from the word *ginomai*, and it describes *a surprising event — something that happens suddenly or unexpectedly and totally takes one off guard.* Here again, we have a description of the rapture of the Church, which will take place in a moment, in the twinkling of an eye. Suddenly, in a split second, the remnant of believers alive on the earth — the restrainer — will be snatched up. The Bible says we will be taken "out of the way," which is a translation of the Greek words *ek mesou.* It means *out of the middle; out of the midst; out of the middle of things.*

If you think about it, the Church is intermingled everywhere throughout the earth. There are believers in government, in the medical field, in the arts, in sports, in the business world — everywhere. We are the temple of the living God (*see* 2 Corinthians 6:16), and everywhere we go we take God's presence. Our very existence on the earth in this present moment is what is restraining the Antichrist from being revealed and rising to power. Once we are raptured, "…then shall that Wicked be revealed…. (2 Thessalonians 2:8).

Putting the meanings of these words together, here is the *Renner Interpretive Version (RIV)* of Second Thessalonians 2:7:

> **These events have been covertly in the making for a long time, but the world doesn't realize that a secret plan is being executed right under their own noses. The only thing that has kept this plan from already being consummated is the supernatural force that has been holding it all back until now. But one day this force will be removed from the picture — and when that happens, these events will quickly transpire.**

What will happen when the Church is evacuated? How will the Antichrist and the energized satanic forces fill the vacuum left behind? That will be our focus in the next lesson.

STUDY QUESTIONS

> Study to shew thyself approved unto God, a workman that needeth
> not to be ashamed, rightly dividing the word of truth.
> — 2 Timothy 2:15

1. Rick mentioned that since the days of the Early Church, Christians have considered five different possibilities for the one that restrains the Antichrist (*see* 2 Thessalonians 2:6,7). Of these five entities, which one(s) had you not heard of? Did you even know there was a *great restrainer*? If so, what have you always understood the restrainer to be?
2. In your own words, describe what the Antichrist will be like when he goes public. In what ways does he remind you of past world leaders that were tyrants? How does he stand in a class all his own?

PRACTICAL APPLICATION

> But be ye doers of the word, and not hearers only,
> deceiving your own selves.
> — James 1:22

1. Before the great *catching away* (the Rapture) of the Church, there must first come a great *falling away*. In Greek, this is the word *apostasia*, and it describes *a mutinous, rebellious attitude toward God*. What are some of the specific things that you have seen in your lifetime that demonstrate this falling away — both in the *world* and in the *Church*?
2. As a part of the Church, you are helping to restrain evil and the coming of the Antichrist. How does this knowledge motivate you to pray and to live? Is there anything you feel compelled to do differently? Is there something you feel encouraged to *start* or *stop* doing?

LESSON 7

TOPIC
What Happens When the Restrainer Is Removed?

SCRIPTURES
1. **2 Thessalonians 2:3-8** — Let no man deceive you by any means: for that day shall not come, except there come a falling away first, and that man of sin be revealed, the son of perdition; Who opposeth and exalteth himself above all that is called God, or that is worshipped; so that he as God sitteth in the temple of God, shewing himself that he is God. Remember ye not, that, when I was yet with you, I told you these things? And now ye know what withholdeth that he might be revealed in his time. For the mystery of iniquity doth already work: only he who now letteth will let, until he be taken out of the way. And then shall that Wicked be revealed, whom the Lord shall consume with the spirit of his mouth, and shall destroy with the brightness of his coming.

GREEK WORDS
1. "deceive" — ἐξαπατάω (*exapatao*): cheat; seduce; to take advantage of by trickery; to deceive by giving distorted impressions; to lure one into deception; to promote delusional thinking and believing using any means
2. "falling away" — ἀποστασία (*apostasia*): a falling away or a revolt; describes political revolt
3. "first" — πρῶτον (*proton*): first in order; in first place
4. "sin" — ἀνομία (*anomia*): lawlessness; without law; a lawless attitude
5. "perdition" — ἀπώλεια (*apoleia*): doomed, rotten, ruinous, or decaying
6. "opposeth" — ἀντίκειμαι (*antikeimai*): opposed to or against everything that is established; a clear reference to the Antichrist
7. "exalteth" — ὑπεραίρω (*huperairo*): to exalt oneself; to exceedingly exalt oneself; to be exalted highly; the idea of one being too highly exalted

8. "above" — ἐπί (*epi*): above; over; implies a position of superiority
9. "all" — πάντα (*panta*): all, nothing excluded
10. "sitteth" — καθίζω (*kathidzo*): to sit down; to be seated
11. "temple" — ναός (*naos*): a temple or a highly decorated shrine; the most sacred, innermost part of a temple; the holy of holies
12. "shewing" — ἀποδείκνυμι (*apodeiknumi*): refers to something outwardly observable or done visibly to authenticate, prove, or guarantee a claim to onlookers; to prove by showing; to display; to show off; used in the Gospels to depict supernatural proof to authenticate the message being preached was true; to make a vivid presentation; to demonstrate
13. "now" — νῦν (*nun*): now, at this very moment in time
14. "withholdeth" — κατέχω (*katecho*): to hold fast; to hold down; to hold back; to suppress; to restrain; to hinder
15. "revealed" — ἀποκάλυψις (*apokalupsis*): to uncover, reveal, or unveil; something that has been veiled or hidden, but suddenly it becomes clear and visible to see; a sudden revealing; when the veil is removed, what was hidden comes into plain view; what is behind the veil is no longer concealed or hidden from private or public view
16. "in his time" — ἐν τῷ ἑαυτοῦ καιρῷ (*en to heautou kairo*): the word καιρός (*kairos*) denotes a specific season or an opportunity
17. "mystery" — μυστήριον (*musterion*): a mystery or secret; once hidden, but now revealed; that which can only be known through revelation
18. "iniquity" — ἀνομία (*anomia*): lawlessness; without law; a lawless attitude
19. "already" — ἤδη (*ede*): no new development, but something that has been at work for quite some time
20. "work" — ἐνεργέω (*energeo*): energized to fulfillment; energized and executed; depicts a force propelling something forward and facilitating it all the way to its conclusion
21. "only" — μόνον (*monon*): alone; only
22. "now" — ἄρτι (*arti*): now; just now; at this moment; in the immediate present
23. "letteth" — κατέχω (*katecho*): to hold fast; to hold down; to hold back; to suppress; to restrain; to hinder
24. "will let" — κατέχω (*katecho*): to hold fast; to hold down; to hold back; to suppress; to restrain; to hinder

25. "until" — ἕως (*heos*): until that moment
26. "be taken" — γένηται (*genetai*): from γίνομαι (*ginomai*); suddenly; unexpectedly; by surprise
27. "out of the way" — ἐκ μέσου (*ek mesou*): out of the middle; out of the midst; out of the middle of things
28. "then" — τότε (*tote*): then; exactly at that time
29. "Wicked" — ὁ ἄνομος (*ho anomos*): the Wicked One; the Lawless One
30. "consume" — ἀναιρέω (*anaireo*): to kill; to murder; to slay; to slaughter; to do away with or abolish
31. "with the spirit" — τῷ πνεύματι (*to pneumati*): spirit; breath
32. "destroy" — καταργέω (*katargeo*): to bring to nothing; to reduce to waste; to render inactive; to abolish; to put out of commission
33. "brightness" — ἐπιφάνεια (*epiphaneia*): a sudden appearance; where we get the word "epiphany"
34. "coming" — παρουσία (*parousia*): a technical expression for the royal visit of a king or emperor; to be present; to arrive or to enter a situation; pictures the arrival of one who alone can deal with a situation

SYNOPSIS

The young believers in the church of Thessalonica were very distraught by an inaccurate letter they had received — possibly from someone they highly respected. They were told that the rapture of the Church had already taken place and that they had been left behind. To calm their fears and dispel the lies they were believing, the apostle Paul wrote to them and said, "Let no man deceive you by any means: for that day [which referred to the Rapture] shall not come, except there come a falling away first, and that man of sin be revealed, the son of perdition" (2 Thessalonians 2:3).

The emphasis of this lesson:

The Bible also refers to the Antichrist as the Wicked One. When Christ returns in the fullness of His glory at the end of the tribulation, He will utterly annihilate the Wicked One with one breath from His mouth.

The Greek word for "no man" in Second Thessalonians 2:3 is a strong prohibition that means, *"Don't let anyone — regardless of who it is — deceive you by teaching that which is not scripturally sound."* The word "deceive" is the Greek word *exapatao*, which means *to cheat, seduce, to take advantage of by trickery*. It can also mean *to deceive by giving distorted impressions, or to lure one into deception*. Whoever wrote the Thessalonian believers may have been sincere in their efforts, but they were promoting delusional thinking and believing. Consequently, their erroneous teaching instilled fear in the hearers.

The rapture had not taken place, and Paul let the Thessalonians know this by saying, "…That day shall not come, except there come a falling away first…" (2 Thessalonians 2:3). Before the rapture takes place, there must be a "falling away." We have seen that this is the Greek word *apostasia*, and it describes *a falling away* or *a revolt*. Plutarch used this word to describe *a political mutiny or revolt*. It also appears in the Septuagint version of the Old Testament in Joshua 22:22 where it describes *a rebellion against the Lord*. In Second Thessalonians 2:3, Paul used this word to denote a worldwide mutinous attitude that will reach an all-time high just before Christ returns. The fact that Paul included the Greek word *proton* — translated here as "first" — tells us that the *apostasia* will be *first in order, first in the sequence of events* to take place.

What Will the Antichrist Be Like Once He's Revealed?

In Second Thessalonians 2:3, Paul assigned two names to the Antichrist. The first is the "Man of Sin." The word *sin* in Greek is *anomia*, which describes *lawlessness*. It carries the idea of *one who has thrown off the past standards of society and no longer wants to live by God's law*. Paul also described the Antichrist as the "Son of Perdition." The word *perdition* is the Greek word *apoleia*, which describes *something doomed, rotten, or ruinous*. It is the same word used to describe *decaying meat filled with maggots*. So while the Antichrist will portray himself as a progressive thinker and framer of the new world order that is free from the standards of Scripture, the fact is, everything he touches will be filled with *rottenness* and *decay*.

What else will the Antichrist do? The Bible says he will "…opposeth and exalteth himself above all that is called God, or that is worshipped…" (2 Thessalonians 2:4). We've seen that the word "opposeth" is the Greek word *antikeimai*, which means *one that is opposed to or against everything that was previously established*. Thus, the Antichrist will try to wipe out all past norms, and at the same time exalt himself above all that is called

God. The word "exalteth" means *to exceedingly exalt oneself* or *to exalt oneself too highly*. The Greek word for "above" is the word *epi*, and it describes *a position of superiority*. The Antichrist is going to elevate himself above "… all that is called God, or that is worshipped…" (2 Thessalonians 2:4). The word "all" is the Greek word *panta*, which literally means *everything*. This means that while he is against Christianity in particular, he will also exalt himself above all world religions.

But that's not all. The Bible also says the Man of Sin will "…sitteth in the temple of God, shewing himself that he is God" (2 Thessalonians 2:4). The word "sitteth" is the Greek word *kathizó*, which means *to sit down* or *to be permanently seated*. Where will he attempt to seat himself? The Bible says "in the temple of God." The word "temple" in Greek is the word *naon*, which is the same word used in the Old Testament Septuagint to describe *the most sacred, innermost part of a temple; the Holy of Holies*. The use of this word implies that the Antichrist will likely enter into a rebuilt temple in Jerusalem and walk into the Holies of Holies and be seated in the place that is God's alone.

Once seated, the Bible says the Antichrist will be "…shewing himself that he is God" (2 Thessalonians 2:4). In Greek, the word "shewing" is *apodeiknumi*, and it depicts *something outwardly observable or done visibly to authenticate, prove, or guarantee a claim to onlookers*. This word is used particularly in the New Testament to describe *signs* and *wonders* or *supernatural activity*. Its use here tells us that the Antichrist will be demonically energized and perform lying signs and wonders to give supernatural proof that authenticates he is God.

Putting the meanings of these words together, here is the *Renner Interpretive Version (RIV)* of Second Thessalonians 2:4:

> **Do you understand who I am talking about? I'm describing that person who will be so against God and everything connected with the worship of God that, if you can imagine it, he will even try to put himself on a pedestal above God Himself — sitting in God's rightful place in the temple and publicly proclaiming himself to be God!**

The Church Is Holding Back the Antichrist from Coming

In Second Thessalonians 2:5, Paul began to remind the Thessalonian believers of what he had told them previously, saying, "Remember ye not, that, when I was yet with you, I told you these things?" Then in verse 6, he said, "And now ye know what withholdeth that he might be revealed in his time." We've seen that the word "withholdeth" is the Greek word *katecho*, which means *to hold fast; to hold down; to hold back; to suppress; to restrain; to hinder*. Paul is letting us know that God has set a supernatural force in the earth that is so strong it is holding back the manifestation of the Antichrist.

This "great restrainer," as some theologians have called it, has been at work since the New Testament times until now. When the restrainer is removed, the Antichrist will "…be revealed in his time." The word "revealed" is the Greek word *apokalupsis*, which means *to uncover, reveal, or unveil*. It depicts *something that has been veiled or hidden, but suddenly it becomes clear and visible to see*. The Church is the restrainer, and when Jesus comes to rapture His people, the veil will be removed. Then the Antichrist — the Man of Lawlessness who has been hidden — will suddenly come into plain view for all to see.

The word "time" in verse 6 is the Greek word *kairos*, which denotes *a specific season* or *an opportunity*. Hence, a specific moment of time is coming when the Antichrist, who has been cleverly concealed from everyone's view, will step out of the shadows and into the light. He will seize the opportunity and begin to lead the world into rebellion against the One True God during the great Tribulation.

Putting the meanings of these words together, here is the *Renner Interpretive Version (RIV)* of Second Thessalonians 2:6:

> **Now in light of everything I've told you before, you ought to be well aware by now that there is a supernatural force at work that is preventing the materialization of this person and the disclosure of his identity. This restraining force I'm referring to is so strong that it is currently putting on the brakes and holding back the unveiling of this wicked person, stalling and postponing his manifestation. But when the right moment comes, this evil one will no longer be withheld, and he will**

emerge on the world scene! The screen that has been hiding his true identity and guarding him from world view will suddenly be pulled back and evaporate — and he will step out on center stage to let everyone know who he is.

Society Is Primed and Prepared To Receive the Lawless One

The apostle Paul continued in Second Thessalonians 2:7, saying, "For the mystery of iniquity doth already work: only he who now letteth will let, until he be taken out of the way." The word "mystery" is the old Greek word *musterion*, and it describes *something that is hidden*. It is *a mystery* or *secret plan; something that was held in the hands of a select few*. In order to have access to such information, a person had to be initiated into the inner circle.

Paul called this the mystery of "iniquity." Here again, we see the Greek word *anomia* — the same word translated as "sin" in Second Thessalonians 2:3. It is derived from the word *nomos*, which means *law*. But when an "a" is attached at the front, it becomes *anomia*, meaning *without law* or *lawlessness*. To be clear, *lawlessness* doesn't necessarily mean chaotic or riotous. It simply depicts a society that has thrown off the high standards and morals it once had — an abandonment of the voice of God and His Word. Indeed, the last day's society will construct a brave new world in which there will be few — if any — hard and fast rules of what is right and wrong.

The Bible says this hidden plan of lawlessness is already at work. The word "already" is the Greek word *ede*, which means *no new development; something that has been at work for quite some time*. And the word "work" is the Greek word *energeo*, which means *energized to fulfillment; something that is energized and executed*. It depicts *a force propelling something forward and facilitating it all the way to its conclusion*. You don't need to look long or hard to see that the current trend of lawlessness in the world has been around for a long time. Satan and his hellish hordes have been working tirelessly for 2,000 years to prepare the world for the Antichrist. Today, we are at a place in history where we have never been. Fear is a constant companion, and society is in search for someone who has the answers for our ailing condition. Indeed, the people are primed and prepared to receive the Man of Lawlessness.

The Mighty Force Insulating Humanity From Evil Is the Church

If we go a little further in Second Thessalonians 2:7, we see that Paul talked again about the supernatural restraining force in the earth. He said, "...Only he who now letteth will let, until he be taken out of the way." The word "only" is the Greek word *monon*, which means *alone; only; no one else*. And the word "now" is the Greek word *arti*, which means *right now; at this moment; in the immediate present*. The combined meaning of these two words lets us know that there is *only one restraining force at this very moment* holding back the mystery of iniquity from being fully set in motion and the Antichrist from being revealed.

Interestingly, the words "letteth" and "let" are the same Greek word repeated twice. It is the word *katecho*, which means *to hold fast; to hold down; to hold back; to suppress; to restrain; to hinder*. This same word appears just one verse earlier and is translated as "withholdeth." What is this supernatural restrainer holding back the forces of evil from taking full control? What is stalling, postponing, and continuing to delay Satan from unveiling the Son of Perdition? Who has been on the earth at work since the New Testament days until now insulating humanity from being totally consumed by evil? It is *the Church*. The Spirit of God working through the Church has been — and continues to be — a mighty force to be reckoned with!

How long will the Antichrist remain hidden? Paul said, "...until he [the restrainer] be taken out of the way" (2 Thessalonians 2:7). In Greek, the word "until" is the Greek word *heos*, and it means *until that precise moment*. The phrase "be taken" in Greek is *genetai*, which is a form of the word *ginomai*, and it describes *something that happens suddenly, unexpectedly, or by surprise*. Once more we see a description of the rapture of the Church, which will take place in a moment, in the twinkling of an eye. The Bible says that suddenly, the remnant of believers alive on the earth will be taken "out of the way." This phrase is a translation of the Greek words *ek mesou*, which means *out of the middle* or *out of the midst of everything*.

Putting the meanings of these words together, here is the *Renner Interpretive Version (RIV)* of Second Thessalonians 2:7:

> **These events have been covertly in the making for a long time, but the world doesn't realize that a secret plan is being executed**

right under their own noses. The only thing that has kept this plan from already being consummated is the supernatural force that has been holding it all back until now. But one day this force will be removed from the picture — and when that happens, these events will quickly transpire.

Christ Will Consume the Wicked One With One Breath from His Mouth

In Second Thessalonians 2:8, Paul went on to tell us, "And then shall that Wicked be revealed, whom the Lord shall consume with the spirit of his mouth, and shall destroy with the brightness of his coming." The word "then" in this verse is the Greek word *tote*, which indicates *then; exactly at that time*. At *the exact moment* when the Church is raptured, then "that Wicked" will be revealed. In Greek, the word "Wicked" is *ho anomos*, meaning *the Wicked One; the Lawless One*. The inclusion of this word tells us that this is not just your average evil person; he is the epitome of wickedness himself. And he will take center stage once the Church is evacuated.

Paul goes on to say, "…The Lord shall consume [him] with the spirit of his mouth…" (2 Thessalonians 2:8). The word "consume" here is *anaireo* in Greek, which means *to kill; to murder; to slay; to slaughter; to do away with,* or *abolish*. How will Jesus "consume" the Antichrist? The Bible says, "with the spirit of his mouth." In Greek, the phrase "with the spirit" is *to pneumatic,* and it means *spirit* or *breath*. A better translation of this would be "with one puff from His mouth." That is how powerful the Word of God is when it comes from the mouth of Jesus!

At the end of the seven-year tribulation, Christ will return to the earth in the fullness of His glory with all believers and settle the score with the Son of Perdition. With one puff of breath from His mouth, Scripture says He will consume the Antichrist, "…and shall destroy [him] with the brightness of his coming" (2 Thessalonians 2:8). The word "destroy" is the Greek word *katargeo,* which means *to bring to nothing; to reduce to waste; to render inactive; to abolish; to put out of commission*. The word "brightness" is a translation of the Greek word *epiphaneia,* and it describes *a sudden appearance*. It is where we get the word "*epiphany.*" This word suggests that when Christ arrives on the scene and opens His mouth, it will be an *epiphany* moment for the Antichrist. Instantly, he will know his life and ruinous rule have come to an end.

It will be the brightness of Jesus' "coming" that will seal his fate. This word "coming" is the same Greek word we saw in Second Thessalonians 2:1 — the word *parousia*. Again, this is *a technical expression for the royal visit of a king or emperor* who has come with all the power, might, and authority to deal with a situation and put everything in order.

Putting the meanings of these words together, here is the *Renner Interpretive Version (RIV)* of Second Thessalonians 2:8:

> **The removal of this restraining force will signal the moment when the Lawless One will finally make his grand appearance to the world — and not too long after that, the Lord will come. His coming will be so grand, so glorious, so overwhelming that He will totally obliterate the Lawless One by the mere breath of His mouth. Just one puff from the Lord, and this evil person will be incinerated! The very presence of the Lord will cripple and immobilize him, permanently putting him out of commission**

In our next lesson, we will identify the energizing force behind the Antichrist and uncover the methods he will use to successfully deceive the masses into believing that he is God.

STUDY QUESTIONS

> Study to shew thyself approved unto God, a workman that needeth not to be ashamed, rightly dividing the word of truth.
> — 2 Timothy 2:15

In Luke 17:26-30, Jesus painted a picture of what the world will be like just before the rapture, comparing it to the "days of Noah" and the "days of Lot." Stop and think.

1. What were the people and the conditions of the world like in the *days of Noah*? (Check out Genesis 6:1-13.)
2. How about the *days of Lot*? What were they like? (Check out Genesis 19:1-29; Ezekiel 16:49,50.) Why do you think Jesus said, "Remember Lot's wife"? (Luke 17:32) How are her actions a picture of some believers in the last days?

3. In what ways are our present days similar to the days of Noah and Lot?

PRACTICAL APPLICATION

> But be ye doers of the word, and not hearers only, deceiving your own selves.
> —James 1:22

1. A careful study of Scripture reveals that the great restrainer holding back the Antichrist and the onslaught of evil in the world is *the Church*. Imagine, what do you think the world will be like *after* the rapture? How difficult do you think it will be for people to serve the Lord? How does this move you to reach out to the lost?
2. First Thessalonians 2:8 says that Jesus will consume the Antichrist with one puff of breath from His mouth! How does this expand your perception of Jesus' power? How does this motivate you to run to Him for help with your struggles with sin? (Consider Hebrews 2:18; 4:15,16.)

LESSON 8

TOPIC
Jesus Will Destroy the Antichrist

SCRIPTURES
1. **2 Thessalonians 2:8-12** — And then shall that Wicked be revealed, whom the Lord shall consume with the spirit of his mouth, and shall destroy with the brightness of his coming: even him, whose coming is after the working of Satan with all power and signs and lying wonders, and with all deceivableness of unrighteousness in them that perish; because they received not the love of the truth, that they might be saved. And for this cause God shall send them strong delusion, that they should believe a lie: That they all might be damned who believed not the truth, but had pleasure in unrighteousness.

GREEK WORDS

1. "then" — τότε (*tote*): then; exactly at that time
2. "Wicked" — ὁ ἄνομος (*ho anomos*): the Wicked One; the Lawless One
3. "revealed" — ἀποκάλυψις (*apokalupsis*): to uncover, reveal, or unveil; something that has been veiled or hidden, but suddenly it becomes clear and visible to see; a sudden revealing; when the veil is removed, what was hidden comes into plain view; what is behind the veil is no longer concealed or hidden from private or public view
4. "consume" — ἀναιρέω (*anaireo*): to kill; to murder; to slay; to slaughter; to do away with or abolish
5. "with the spirit" — τῷ πνεύματι (*to pneumati*): spirit; breath
6. "destroy" — καταργέω (*katargeo*): to bring to nothing; to reduce to waste; to render inactive; to abolish; to put out of commission
7. "coming" — παρουσία (*parousia*): a technical expression for the royal visit of a king or emperor; to be present, to arrive, or to enter a situation in order to put everything in order
8. "brightness" — ἐπιφάνεια (*epiphaneia*): a sudden appearance; where we get the word "epiphany"
9. "coming" — παρουσία (*parousia*): a technical expression for the royal visit of a king or emperor
10. "after" — κατ' (*kat'*): dominated or subjugated
11. "working" — ἐνέργεια (*energeia*): being energized to fulfillment; energized and executed; depicts a force propelling something forward or an energy that ignites a process and facilitating it all the way to its conclusion
12. "Satan" — Σατανᾶς (*Satanas*): one who conspires against
13. "with all" — ἐν πάσῃ (*en pase*): in all; with all kinds
14. "power" — δύναμις (*dunamis*): power; supernatural power; the full force of an advancing army; where we get the word "dynamite"
15. "signs" — σημεῖον (*semeion*): plural, a sign, a mark, or a token to authenticate a thing; an act that points the viewer in a certain direction or an action performed to prove a point; used in the New Testament to depict miracles and supernatural events
16. "and" — καί (*kai*): and; even

17. "lying" — ψεῦδος (*pseudos*): falsehood; picture one who projects a false image of himself; one who deliberately walks in a pretense that is untrue or intentionally misrepresents facts or truths; something bogus
18. "wonders" — τέρας (*teras*): plural; an event that leaves one baffled, bewildered, astonished, at a loss of words; depicts shock, surprise, or astonishment felt by bystanders who observed events that were contrary to the course of nature; events so shocking that they left spectators speechless, taken aback, stunned, awestruck, and in a state of wonder
19. "with all" — ἐν πάσῃ (*en pase*): with all kinds
20. "deceivableness" — ἀπάτη (*apate*): a deliberate seduction or deception; a meticulously planned deception intended to lead a person or entire race into error; intentional trickery designed to deceive, seduce, and mislead
21. "perish" — ἀπόλλυμι (*apollumi*): to undo; to destroy; to permanently perish; pictures total devastation and complete ruin; destruction and waste
22. "received" [not]: δέχομαι (*dechomai*): to take into one's hands; to receive with gladness
23. "saved" — σῴζω (*sodzo*): saved for eternal life; includes healing or wholeness in every part of life; to protect or keep safe; to keep under protection; being kept from evil or being saved; rescued from harm, or delivered from danger
24. "and for this cause" — καὶ διὰ τοῦτο (*kai dia touto*): for this reason; pictures God's response to their choice
25. "strong delusion" — ἐνέργειαν πλάνης (*energeian planes*): the word ἐνεργέω (*energeo*) and πλάνη (*plane*) the word ἐνεργέω (*energeo*) depicts a force propelling something forward or an energy that ignites a process and facilitates it all the way to its conclusion; the word πλάνη (*plane*) pictures wandering or deviant behavior; to leave a solid moral path; used to depict an animal that lost its way and could never find its way back home
26. "damned" — κρίνω (*krino*): judgment or a sentence; the condemning sentence of a court

SYNOPSIS

In our previous lessons, we learned that the Church is the great restrainer holding back the powers of darkness in the world and keeping the Antichrist from being revealed. But there is coming a moment in the near future when the restrainer will be removed. That is, the Church will be raptured right out of the middle of everything. The moment we are evacuated, the Antichrist will immediately rise to power, seizing his long-awaited opportunity to lead the world into doom, decay, and destruction.

The emphasis of this lesson:

During the tribulation, the Antichrist will be dominated and energized by Satan himself and quickly rise to the level of emperor over the earth. Through supernatural signs and lying wonders, he will successfully deceive the masses into believing the lie that he is God. Those who swallow his lie and reject the truth will forfeit their chance to be saved.

A Review of Second Thessalonians 2:8

When the Church has been removed from the earth, the Bible says, "And then shall that Wicked be revealed, whom the Lord shall consume with the spirit of his mouth, and shall destroy with the brightness of his coming" (2 Thessalonians 2:8). The word "then" here is the Greek word *tote*, and it means *then; exactly at that time*. At *the precise moment* when the Church is raptured, "…then shall that Wicked be revealed…."

"**Revealed**" is the Greek word *apokalupsis*, which means *to uncover, reveal, or unveil; a sudden revealing*. It depicts something that has been veiled or hidden suddenly becoming clear and visible to see. When the veil is removed, what was hidden comes into plain view; what is behind the veil is no longer concealed or hidden from private or public view. When the Church is evacuated, the identity of the Antichrist will be visible for all to see for the first time.

"**That Wicked**" in verse 8 is the Greek word *ho anomos*. What is interesting is that Wicked is capitalized, indicating he is *the Wicked One* or *the Lawless One*. This word is taken from the word *anomia*, the word for *lawlessness*, and it depicts *one who refuses to acknowledge and submit to the law of God*. Although the Antichrist will portray himself as a progressive thinker who will turn the world into a paradise of peace, his efforts will produce a rottenness in society that is beyond comprehension.

Writing under the inspiration of the Holy Spirit, Paul then prophesied the future of the Antichrist, saying, "...The Lord shall consume [him] with the spirit of his mouth..." (2 Thessalonians 2:8). First, notice the word "Lord." It is the Greek word *Kurios*, and in this verse it is capitalized, which means this is not just any lord. This is *THE Lord of all lords* — the greatest of them all! When Jesus arrives on the scene, He will "consume" the Antichrist.

"**Consume**" in Greek is the word *anaireo*, which means *to kill; to murder; to slay; to slaughter; to do away with or abolish*. How will Christ accomplish this annihilation? The Bible says, "with the spirit of his mouth." In Greek, the phrase "with the spirit" is *to pneumatic*, and it denotes *spirit* or *breath*. A better translation of this part of the verse would be, "With one small puff of breath from the mouth of Jesus, He will destroy the Antichrist."

As the seven-year tribulation reaches its conclusion, Christ will come again in all His glory "...and shall destroy [the Antichrist] with the brightness of his coming" (2 Thessalonians 2:8). In Greek, the word "**destroy**" is *katargeo*, which means *to bring to nothing; to reduce to waste; to render inactive; to abolish;* or *to put out of commission*.

It will be the brightness of Jesus' "coming" that will effectively defeat the Antichrist. The Greek word for "**coming**" is *parousia* — the same word we saw in Second Thessalonians 2:1. Once more, this is *a technical expression for the royal visit of a king or emperor* who has come with all the power, might, and authority to deal with a situation and put everything in order.

"**Brightness**" is also a significant word. It is the Greek term *epiphaneia*, and it describes *a sudden, unexpected appearance*. It is where we get the word *"epiphany,"* and its use here indicates that when Christ arrives on the scene and speaks the Word, it will be an *epiphany* moment for the Antichrist that permanently takes him out of commission.

Putting the meanings of these words together, here is the *Renner Interpretive Version (RIV)* of Second Thessalonians 2:8:

> **The removal of this restraining force will signal the moment when the Lawless One will finally make his grand appearance to the world — and not too long after that, the Lord will come. His coming will be so grand, so glorious, so overwhelming that He will totally obliterate the Lawless One by the mere breath of His mouth. Just one puff from the Lord, and this evil**

person will be incinerated! The very presence of the Lord will cripple and immobilize him, permanently putting him out of commission

The Antichrist's Coming Will Be 'After the Working of Satan'

In Second Thessalonians 2:9, the apostle Paul described what the rule of the Antichrist will be like during the tribulation: "Even him, whose coming is after the working of Satan with all power and signs and lying wonders." Here again we see the word "coming"— the Greek word *parousia*. Remember, it is a technical expression for *the royal visit of a king or emperor*. Only in this verse it is referring to the Antichrist, not Jesus. The fact that this word is included here tells us that during the tribulation, the Antichrist will rise to the level of a worldwide king or emperor, literally ruling the planet for seven years.

The Bible says his coming is "…after the working of Satan…." The word "after" is the Greek word *kat*, which always carries the idea of being *dominated* or *subjugated*. This tells us clearly that Satan himself will *dominate* the Antichrist. Everything he does will be the "working" of Satan. In Greek, the word "working" is *energeia*, which means *being energized to fulfillment*. It depicts *a force propelling something forward or to the front*. This lets us know that Satan will energize the Antichrist and propel him out in front of everybody.

That brings us to the word "Satan"— the Greek word *Satanas*, which always describes *one who conspires against*. We saw in our previous lesson that there actually is a conspiracy at work in the world today. It has been developing since the days of the Early Church. Paul called it the "mystery of iniquity." It is Satan's secret plan to slowly but surely modify the world into a state of lawlessness so that it is primed and prepared to embrace the Man of Lawlessness with open arms. The fact that the Antichrist's coming will be "after the working of Satan" tells us that Satan will finally achieve and bring to a conclusion what he has been striving for all along.

He Will Produce Supernatural 'Signs and Lying Wonders'

What will be the result of the Antichrist being demonically energized? Paul said he will come "…with all power and signs and lying wonders"

(2 Thessalonians 2:9). The phrase "with all" in Greek means *with all kinds*. The word "power" is the Greek word *dunamis*, which is the same word used to describe the "power" of the Holy Spirit (*see* Acts 1:8) and the "power" of the Gospel (*see* Romans 1:16). The word *dunamis* describes *supernatural power* and indicates *the full force of an advancing army*. It is where we get the word "dynamite." Normally, this is a wonderfully inspiring word. However, in this verse it denotes demonic supernatural activity that will flow through the Antichrist.

Specifically, Paul said he would produce "signs." In Greek, the word for "signs" is *semeion*, which describes *a sign, a mark, or a token to authenticate a thing; an act that points the viewer in a certain direction or an action performed to prove a point*. This word was used in the New Testament to depict *miracles* and *supernatural events* that validated the message of the Gospel.

Paul said the Antichrist would employ signs "and lying wonders." What's interesting here is that the word "and" is also important. It is the Greek word *kai*, which would better be translated as *even*. Thus, Paul said, "and even lying wonders." The word "lying" in Greek is *pseudos*, which means *falsehood*. It is a picture of *one who projects a false image of himself; one who deliberately walks in a pretense that is untrue or intentionally misrepresents facts or truths; something bogus*.

The word "wonders" is a translation of the Greek word *teras*, which describes *an event that leaves one baffled, bewildered, astonished, or at a loss of words*. It can also depict *shock, surprise, or astonishment felt by bystanders who observed events that were contrary to the course of nature*. In this case, these events will be so shocking that they will leave spectators speechless, taken aback, stunned, awestruck, and in a state of wonder. This confirms what we learned in Second Thessalonians 2:4 — that the Antichrist will seat himself in the Holy of Holies of God's temple and show himself to be God through a display of supernatural activity. But every sign and lying wonder he performs will be energized by Satan and demonic forces.

Putting the meanings of these words together, here is the *Renner Interpretive Version (RIV)* of Second Thessalonians 2:9:

> **This evil one will be energized by Satan himself as he makes his arrival known to the world with all kinds of dynamic supernatural powers that are truly extraordinary. These lying signs and wonders and supernatural feats have only one purpose: they are**

designed to draw attention to the Lawless One and to make the world stand in awe of him.

Those Who Reject the Truth Forfeit Their Chance To Be Saved

Then in Second Thessalonians 2:10, Paul continues to describe the way the Antichrist will work, saying, "And with all deceivableness of unrighteousness in them that perish; because they received not the love of the truth, that they might be saved." Once more we see the phrase "with all," which means *with all kinds*. This indicates the Antichrist will use *all kinds* of methods to successfully seduce and deceive the people into believing he is God.

The word "deceivableness" is the Greek word *apate*, and it describes *a deliberate seduction or deception; a meticulously planned deception intended to lead a person or entire race into error*. This trickery is intentionally designed to deceive, seduce, and mislead. Energized by Satan, the Antichrist will lead the inhabitants of the world into a web of seduction. And the Bible specifically notes "…them that perish…" (2 Thessalonians 2:10). In Greek, the word "perish" is *apollumi*, which means *to undo; to destroy; to permanently perish*. It pictures *total devastation and complete ruin; destruction and waste*.

The word *apollumi* — translated here as "perish" — is very important because it describes what happens to an individual who rejects the truth. Ultimately, they are not destroyed by God, but by their own choices. This verse states that "…because they received not the love of the truth, that they might be saved" (2 Thessalonians 2:10). In Greek, the word "received" is *dechomai*, which means *to take into one's hands; to receive with gladness*. This indicates that the message of the Gospel was presented to these individuals, and they had the opportunity to accept it. Instead, they chose to reject it.

Putting the meanings of these words together, here is the *Renner Interpretive Version (RIV)* of Second Thessalonians 2:10:

> He will do anything to seduce people — exploiting them with illusions, tricks, and all types of unrighteousness that are designed to deceive and seduce the masses. But these supernatural tricks will primarily be targeted to those who are perishing

— those who had the chance to embrace the love of the truth, but who didn't take the opportunity when it was presented to them. They refused the truth and have therefore forfeited their chance to be rescued, saved, and delivered.

Truth Rejectors Will Be Ensnared by a 'Strong Delusion'

What happens to these individuals who reject the love of the truth? Paul tells us, "And for this cause God shall send them strong delusion, that they should believe a lie" (2 Thessalonians 2:11). In Greek, the phrase "and for this cause" is *kai dia touto*, which means *for this reason*, and it pictures *God's response to their choice*. Please know that God is not in a rush, nor does He want, to send delusion to anyone. The Bible says He "…is longsuffering to us-ward, not willing that any should perish, but that all should come to repentance" (2 Peter 3:9).

Nevertheless, God has given everyone a free will and will let us have what we want. If people choose to believe a lie instead of the truth, He will let them. He will even allow the lie to run its full course in their life if they so desire. Why? Because He will not force His will on anyone.

The Bible says those who willfully choose to believe a lie will be sent "strong delusion." This phrase is a translation of the Greek words *energeian planes*, which has a very unique meaning. It is derived from the words *energeo* and *plane*. The word *energeo* depicts *a force propelling something forward or an energy that ignites a process and facilitates it all the way to its conclusion*. And the word *plane* pictures *wandering or deviant behavior*; it means *to leave a solid, moral path* and was used to depict an animal that lost its way and could never find its way back home. The use of the phrase *energeian planes* means those who believe the lie of the Antichrist will be demonically energized by deception. Specifically, they will be energized to believe the lie they have embraced.

Putting the meanings of these words together, here is the *Renner Interpretive Version (RIV)* of Second Thessalonians 2:11:

> **Because they chose to reject the truth, God will send delusion and error into their midst, compelling them to believe the lie that is being offered to them [by the Antichrist].**

And They Had Pleasure in Unrighteousness

The apostle Paul wrapped up his description of what is going to happen to those who reject the truth in Second Thessalonians 2:12, saying, "That they all might be damned who believed not the truth, but had pleasure in unrighteousness." The word "damned" here is actually not a good translation. It is the Greek word *krino*, which describes *a judgment or a sentence; it is the final verdict of a court*. In this case, it is the condemning sentence of the court of Heaven. After God has examined all the facts and viewed all the evidence presented to Him in the case against sinful humanity, He will issue a guilty verdict at the end of the age.

Putting the meanings of these words together, here is the *Renner Interpretive Version (RIV)* of Second Thessalonians 2:12:

> **God will send a delusion among these truth-rejecters. They could have accepted the truth and believed, but they made the willful decision to participate in and fully enjoy their unrighteous deeds. In the end, they will be thoroughly judged and condemned by their own actions. Because they gave themselves so entirely to the enjoyment of wrongdoing, there will be plenty of evidence to use against them in God's court of law on the day they stand before Him to be judged.**

In our next lesson, we will look back over all we have learned so far from our study on *The Coming of the Antichrist* and see how things fit together with the soon return of Jesus and the rapture of the Church.

STUDY QUESTIONS

> **Study to shew thyself approved unto God, a workman that needeth not to be ashamed, rightly dividing the word of truth.**
> **— 2 Timothy 2:15**

1. Although Jesus said no one would know the *day* or the *hour* of His return (*see* Matthew 24:36), He did say there was something we could and should know about His coming. Read Matthew 24:32-34 and identify the "lesson from the fig tree" He wants us to learn.
2. Along with all that Paul spoke to the Thessalonian believers about the rapture of the Church and the coming of the Antichrist, he also gave them practical instructions for everyday living. What can you per-

sonally take away from his words in First Thessalonians 5:12-22 and apply in your own life?

PRACTICAL APPLICATION

> But be ye doers of the word, and not hearers only,
> deceiving your own selves.
> —James 1:22

1. Rejecting the truth is dangerous. Sometimes we do it unknowingly due to past hurts or fear in our hearts. Be still and ask the Holy Spirit to reveal any area in your life where you have unknowingly rejected the truth and are deluded in your thinking. Repent of anything He shows you, and ask Him for the strength to obey what He is telling you to do.

2. We are living in critical times. The return of Christ is fast approaching. As believers, it is exciting to think about what is ahead, but what about your unsaved family members and friends — and those who've walked away from their devotion to Jesus? Ask the Holy Spirit to give you the opportunity and the right attitude to lovingly yet boldly share the truth of the Gospel with words they can hear and receive.

And pray for them…

- That the Holy Spirit will draw them to Jesus (*see* John 6:44,65).

- To have their eyes open to the truth (*see* Psalm 119:18; Acts 9:18).

- To have a heart of repentance and escape the enemy's snare (*see* 2 Timothy 2:25,26).

- To have the measure of faith needed to believe/receive Jesus as Lord (*see* Romans 12:3).

LESSON 9

TOPIC
Recap: The Coming of the Antichrist

SCRIPTURES
1. **1 Thessalonians 4:15-18** — For this we say unto you by the word of the Lord, that we which are alive and remain unto the coming of the Lord shall not prevent them which are asleep. For the Lord himself shall descend from heaven with a shout, with the voice of the archangel, and with the trump of God: and the dead in Christ shall rise first: Then we which are alive and remain shall be caught up together with them in the clouds, to meet the Lord in the air: and so shall we ever be with the Lord. Wherefore comfort one another with these words.
2. **1 Corinthians 15:51,52** — Behold, I shew you a mystery; We shall not all sleep, but we shall all be changed, in a moment, in the twinkling of an eye, at the last trump: for the trumpet shall sound, and the dead shall be raised incorruptible, and we shall be changed.
3. **2 Thessalonians 2:1-12** — Now we beseech you, brethren, by the coming of our Lord Jesus Christ, and by our gathering together unto him, that ye be not soon shaken in mind, or be troubled, neither by spirit, nor by word, nor by letter as from us, as that the day of Christ is at hand. Let no man deceive you by any means: for that day shall not come, except there come a falling away first, and that man of sin be revealed, the son of perdition. Who opposeth and exalteth himself above all that is called God, or that is worshipped; so that he as God sitteth in the temple of God, shewing himself that he is God. Remember ye not, that, when I was yet with you, I told you these things? And now ye know what withholdeth that he might be revealed in his time. For the mystery of iniquity doth already work: only he who now letteth will let, until he be taken out of the way. And then shall that Wicked be revealed, whom the Lord shall consume with the spirit of his mouth, and shall destroy with the brightness of his coming: Even him, whose coming is after the working of Satan with all power and signs and lying wonders, and with all deceivableness of unrighteousness in them that perish; because they received not the love of the truth, that they might be saved. And for this cause

God shall send them strong delusion, that they should believe a lie: That they all might be damned who believed not the truth, but had pleasure in unrighteousness.

SYNOPSIS

In the previous eight lessons, we have covered a great deal of Bible prophecy. We learned about the rapture of the Church — which explodes into reality with a mighty shout from Jesus, the voice of the archangel, and the sounding of the last trumpet. We examined the physical transformation we are going to experience when the rapture takes place. And we also spent a great deal of time studying the events that are going to occur just before the rapture and just after it, including the coming of the Antichrist and how he will rule during the tribulation and then be utterly destroyed by the brightness of Christ's second coming.

The emphasis of this lesson:

In this lesson, we're going to recap all that we have learned thus far, using the *Renner Interpretive Version (RIV)* of each passage of Scripture. This includes what the return of Christ will look like, the promise of a brand new body, and a portrait of the man of perdition and his prophesied extermination.

What the Return of Christ Will Look Like

In First Thessalonians 4:13-18, the apostle Paul wrote about the coming of the Lord Jesus to encourage the believers who had lost loved ones that had died in their faith. In this passage, which is a blueprint of the blessed hope in Christ, Paul declared:

> "For this we say unto you by the word of the Lord, that we which are alive and remain unto the coming of the Lord shall not prevent them which are asleep. For the Lord himself shall descend from heaven with a shout, with the voice of the archangel, and with the trump of God: and the dead in Christ shall rise first: Then we which are alive and remain shall be caught up together with them in the clouds, to meet the Lord in the air: and so shall we ever be with the Lord. Wherefore comfort one another with these words."
>
> 1 Thessalonians 4:15-18

Verses like these concerning the rapture of the Church should comfort and encourage you, not make you afraid. The greatest event in the history of the Church since Christ's resurrection from the dead and the Day of Pentecost is just ahead, and God wants us to be ready for it. To remind us of the deep meaning of this passage, let's review the *Renner Interpretive Version (RIV)* of First Thessalonians 4:15-18.

Verse 15

For we declare this to you by the word of the Lord, those who are physically alive and who have survived everything — I'm talking about the remaining remnant that will still be left around at the time of the coming of the Lord — that living and surviving remnant will not precede those who have already died.

Verse 16

For the Lord Himself will descend from Heaven to take charge with a mighty military command that will arouse the saints and galvanize God's troops to action. And along with that command, precisely at that time will also be heard the immense voice of an Archangel, along with the blast of God's war trumpet to signal that the final battle, ultimate victory, and vanquishing of all God's enemies is about to occur. That war-trumpet blast will be the indication that God's enemies have lost their longstanding battle with Him and that He reigns victorious and supreme over everyone, over every situation, and over every realm — total victory! And exactly when that war-trumpet sound goes forth, the dead in Christ will immediately stand upright on their feet as they are resurrected to a brand-new, resurrected, royal status. This resurrection will take place as a first priority before the next sequence of events takes place.

Verse 17

Then at that exact synchronized moment, those who are still physically alive and who have survived everything — I'm talking about the remnant that will still be around and left remaining at this time — they will suddenly and supernaturally be snatched away out of imminent danger just in the nick of time as the Lord instigates a divine rescue operation to

transport them into the clouds to join those who have been resurrected. There in the air's lower atmosphere where the Lord has descended to meet them, those who were raised from dead and the remnant who were supernaturally snatched out of danger, will encounter the Lord. And at that encounter, the Lord will roll out the red carpet to give the new arrivals a royal reception to match the VIP status He knows they deserve! Then and after that, we will always — indivisible and forevermore — be with the Lord.

Verse 18
So then, encourage, exhort, positively provoke, rouse, stir up, and spur one another on with these words. Do your best — make it your aim to help each other to stand tall, to throw your shoulders back, to hold your head high, and to bravely face whatever battle or circumstance presents itself to you. Yes, make it your goal to encourage one another with the words that I have written to you.

The rapture of the Church will be a sudden, supernatural snatching away of the remnant of believers who are alive on the earth at the time of His coming. The original Greek indicates this stealth rescue operation will be led by Christ Himself. When it seems as though the world is caving in on Christians, Christ will step into time — raising the dead who believed in Him and making a way of escape for believers who are alive on the earth. What a glorious day that will be! If there was ever a truth we should speak to encourage a fellow believer, this is it.

The Promise of a Brand New Body

When we come to First Corinthians 15:51 and 52, the Holy Spirit speaks through Paul and gives us a more detailed explanation of the physical transformation believers are going to experience at the time of the rapture. He said:

> "Behold, I shew you a mystery; We shall not all sleep, but we shall all be changed, in a moment, in the twinkling of an eye, at the last trump: for the trumpet shall sound, and the dead shall be raised incorruptible, and we shall be changed."
>
> **1 Corinthians 15:51,52**

Putting the meanings of the key words together, here is the *Renner Interpretive Version (RIV)* of First Corinthians 15:51,52:

Verse 51

What I am about to say will totally flabbergast you, but listen carefully, for I am going to tell you something that was previously an unknown mystery, but has now been revealed to us. Here it is: All will not die, but all — the dead and even the living — will be altered, changed, miraculously modified, and transformed.

Verse 52

In a moment — a split second, an indivisible atom of time — as fast as the twitch of an eye, at the very last trump, that war trumpet will loudly sound to signal that the final battle, ultimate victory, and vanquishing of all God's enemies is about to finally happen. That blast will be God's way of letting everyone know that His enemies have lost their footing and longstanding battle with Him and that He reigns victorious and supreme in total victory!

In that flash, the dead will stand upright on their feet and will be resurrected to a brand-new, resurrected, royal status. And at that exact moment, they will miraculously receive new bodies that are incapable of decay and that will never again show the effects of wear, tear, and age — timeless, immortal, indestructible bodies. We who are still alive when all this happens will be supernaturally transformed as our old bodies are exchanged for new ones that also are incapable of decay and that will never again show the effects of wear, tear, and age. Our bodies will literally be altered, changed, miraculously modified, and transformed into timeless, immortal, indestructible bodies.

How amazing! When we combine Paul's words in First Thessalonians chapter 4 and First Corinthians chapter 15, we have a very vivid description of the rapture of the Church and what we expect to take place. These verses are simply undeniable. If someone tells you that there's no rapture, they're ignoring very important biblical passages like these.

A Portrait of the Man of Perdition and His Prophesied Extermination

When we come to Second Thessalonians chapter 2, we see Paul writing to the young believers in Thessalonica to assure them that the rapture of the Church had not taken place as they had erroneously been told. After reminding them of what needed to occur before the rapture, he gave them — *and us* — a prophetic picture of the future regarding the unveiling of the Antichrist and the characteristics of his short-lived reign. He said:

> "Now we beseech you, brethren, by the coming of our Lord Jesus Christ, and by our gathering together unto him, that ye be not soon shaken in mind, or be troubled, neither by spirit, nor by word, nor by letter as from us, as that the day of Christ is at hand. Let no man deceive you by any means: for that day shall not come, except there come a falling away first, and that man of sin be revealed, the son of perdition. Who opposeth and exalteth himself above all that is called God, or that is worshipped; so that he as God sitteth in the temple of God, shewing himself that he is God. Remember ye not, that, when I was yet with you, I told you these things? And now ye know what withholdeth that he might be revealed in his time. For the mystery of iniquity doth already work: only he who now letteth will let, until he be taken out of the way. And then shall that Wicked be revealed, whom the Lord shall consume with the spirit of his mouth, and shall destroy with the brightness of his coming: Even him, whose coming is after the working of Satan with all power and signs and lying wonders, and with all deceivableness of unrighteousness in them that perish; because they received not the love of the truth, that they might be saved. And for this cause God shall send them strong delusion, that they should believe a lie: That they all might be damned who believed not the truth, but had pleasure in unrighteousness."
> — 2 Thessalonians 2:1-12

Putting the meanings of the key words together, here is the *Renner Interpretive Version (RIV)* of Second Thessalonians 2:1-12:

Verse 1

Brothers, listen carefully, for I am asking you in the strongest of terms to hear what I am about to say and to do exactly what I'm asking you to do. The appearance of the Lord Jesus Christ is very near. The moment we have all longed and waited for is almost upon us! I'm talking about that moment when Jesus will finally gather us together for Himself.

Verse 2

Some things will be happening right before His coming that could shake you up quite a bit. I'm referring to events that will be so dramatic that they could leave your head spinning — occurrences of such a serious nature that many people will end up feeling alarmed, panicked, intimidated, and unnerved. Naturally speaking, these events could put your nerves on edge and make you feel apprehensive and insecure. How I wish I could tell you these incidents were going to be just a one-shot deal, but when they finally get rolling, they're going to keep coming and coming, one after another. That's why you have to determine not to be shaken or moved by anything you see or hear. You need to get a grip on your mind and refuse to allow yourselves to be traumatized by these events. If you let these things get to you, it won't be too long until you're a nervous wreck! That's why you have to decide beforehand that you are not going to give in and allow fright to penetrate its way into your mind and emotions until it runs your whole life. I also want to tell you not to be too surprised if people start making weird spiritual proclamations and off-the-wall utterances during the time just before the Lord comes. All kinds of strange things are going to happen during those days! It's going to get so bizarre that you might even receive a letter from some person who claims that the day of the Lord has already come! Who knows — they might even attach our name to it, alleging to have our endorsement. Or they might even send it as if it were written and sent from us.

Verse 3

In light of these things, I urge you to refuse to allow anyone to take advantage of you. For example, you won't need a letter to tell you when the day of the Lord has come. You ought to know by now that this day can't come until first a worldwide insurgency, rebellion, riot, and mutiny against God has come about in society. Once that occurs, the world will be primed, prepared, and ready to embrace the Man of Lawlessness, the one who hates law and has rebellion running in his blood. This is the long-awaited and predicted Son of Doom and Destruction, the one who brings rot and ruin to everything he touches. When the time is just right, he will finally come out of hiding and go public.

Verse 4

Do you understand who I am talking about? I'm describing that person who will be so against God and everything connected with the worship of God that, if you can imagine it, he will even try to put himself on a pedestal above God Himself — sitting in God's rightful place in the temple and publicly proclaiming himself to be God.

Verse 5

Don't you remember that when I was there with you, I used to regularly tell you these things?

Verse 6

Now in light of everything I've told you before, you ought to be well aware by now that there is a supernatural force at work that is preventing the materialization of this person and the disclosure of his identity. This restraining force I'm referring to is so strong that it is currently putting on the brakes and holding back the unveiling of this wicked person, stalling and postponing his manifestation. But when the right moment comes, this evil one will no longer be withheld, and he will emerge on the world scene! The screen that has been hiding his true identity and guarding him from world view will suddenly be pulled back and evaporate — and he will step out on center stage to let everyone know who he is.

Verse 7

These events have been covertly in the making for a long time but the world doesn't realize that a secret plan is being executed right under their own noses. The only thing that has kept this plan from already being consummated is the supernatural force that has been holding it all back until now. But one day this force will be removed from the picture — and when that happens, these events will quickly transpire.

Verse 8

The removal of this restraining force will signal the moment when the Lawless One will finally make his grand appearance to the world — and not too long after that, the Lord will come. His coming will be so grand, so glorious, so overwhelming that He will totally obliterate the Lawless One by the mere breath of His mouth. Just one puff from the Lord, and this evil person will be incinerated! The very presence of the Lord will cripple and immobilize him and permanently put him out of commission.

Verse 9

This evil one will be energized by Satan himself as he makes his arrival known to the world with all kinds of dynamic supernatural powers that will be truly extraordinary. These lying signs and wonders and supernatural feats have only one purpose: they are designed to draw attention to the Lawless One and to make the world stand in awe of him.

Verse 10

He will do anything to seduce people — exploiting them with illusions, tricks, and all types of unrighteousness that are designed to deceive and seduce the masses. But these supernatural tricks will primarily be targeted to those who are perishing — those who had the chance to embrace the love of the truth, but who didn't take the opportunity when it was presented to them. They refused the truth and have therefore forfeited their chance to be rescued, saved, and delivered.

Verse 11

Because they chose to reject the truth, God will send delusion and error into their midst, compelling them to believe the lie that is being offered to them [by the Antichrist].

Verse 12

God will send a delusion among these truth-rejecters. They could have accepted the truth and believed, but they made the willful decision to participate in and fully enjoy their unrighteous deeds. In the end, they will be thoroughly judged and condemned by their own actions. Because they gave themselves so entirely to the enjoyment of wrongdoing, there will be plenty of evidence to use against them in God's court of law on the day they stand before Him to be judged.

Friend, the coming of our Lord Jesus Christ is near! It's closer today than when Paul penned these words nearly 2,000 years ago. The Holy Spirit believed it was important for us to know and understand what is coming in the days ahead — not to scare us, but to prepare us to recognize the sign of the times in which we live and "make the most of every opportunity in these evil days" (Ephesians 5:16 *NLT*).

Clearly, the mutinous, rebellious attitude toward God and all established authority Paul prophesied is already present in the world and rapidly spreading. In our final lesson, we will focus on how we need to personally respond to all the bizarre events taking place in these last of the last days in order to avoid falling into the pitfall of apostasy.

STUDY QUESTIONS

Study to shew thyself approved unto God, a workman that needeth not to be ashamed, rightly dividing the word of truth.
— 2 Timothy 2:15

In Matthew 25:1-13, Jesus compared His sudden, unexpected return — the rapture of the Church — with ten virgins who were waiting for the return of the bridegroom. Take a few moments to carefully read this passage.

1. Knowing that the ten virgins represent members of the Church, how prepared will the Church be when He unexpectedly returns? How prepared are you?
2. What actions did the five *wise* virgins take that Jesus praised?
3. What did the *foolish* virgins fail to do that the wise virgins could not help them with?

4. What wisdom can you take away from this parable and personally apply in your own life?

PRACTICAL APPLICATION

> But be ye doers of the word, and not hearers only, deceiving your own selves.
> —James 1:22

1. After reading through the detailed *Renner Interpretive Version (RIV)* of each section of Scripture, what new insights is the Holy Spirit showing you regarding:
   - The rapture of the Church
   - The rule of the Antichrist
   - The annihilation of the Antichrist

2. To each church in the book of Revelation — and to the Church throughout all generations — Jesus said, "He that hath an ear, let him hear what the Spirit saith unto the churches…" (Revelation 2:7). What can you do on a daily basis to hear more clearly what the Holy Spirit is speaking to *you* as a member of the Church? (Consider Psalm 51:10-12; Romans 12:1,2; Jude 1:20.) How are you encouraged to know that God wants to speak to you and direct you in these last days? (Consider John 16:12-15; Jeremiah 33:3.)

LESSON 10

TOPIC

Guarding Against Apostasy

SCRIPTURES

1. **1 Timothy 4:1** — Now the Spirit speaketh expressly, that in the latter times some shall depart from the faith, giving heed to seducing spirits, and doctrines of devils.

GREEK WORDS

1. "expressly" — ῥητῶς (*rhetos*): unmistakably; vividly; pictures something spoken clearly or something that is unquestionable, certain, and sure
2. "latter" — ὕστερος (*husteros*): latter; pictures the ultimate end or the very last of something
3. "depart" — ἀφίστημι (*aphistemi*): compound of ἀπό (*apo*) and ἵστημι (*histimi*); the word ἀπό (*apo*) means away; the word ἵστημι (*histimi*) means to stand; compounded, the word ἀφίστημι (*aphistemi*) means to stand apart from; to distance one's self from; to step away from; to withdraw from; or to shrink away from; it is from this very Greek word that we derive the word apostate or apostasy
4. "the faith" — πίστεως (*pisteos*): refers to doctrine or to the long-held, time-tested teachings of Scripture
5. "giving heed" — προσέχω (*prosecho*): to turn in a new direction; to embrace
6. "seducing" — πλανάω (*planao*): to wander; pictures deception, moral wandering, deviant behavior; a person (or nation) that has veered from a solid path; as a result of veering morally, this person is adrift; also used to depict a lost animal that cannot find its path; to morally lose one's bearings; to wander off course
7. "doctrines" — διδασκαλία (*didaskalia*): well-packaged teaching that is applicable to lifestyle
8. "devils" — δαιμόνιον (*daimonion*): in context, evil spirits, demons, devils; the ancient world believed demons thickly populated the lower regions of the air and that spirits were the primary cause of disasters, suffering, and actions of insanity

SYNOPSIS

Can you feel it in your spirit? The signs are all around us. Christ is about ready to rapture the Church right out of the middle of everything! Although we can't know the day or the hour, Jesus said we can — and *should* — know the season of His return. As soon as the Church is evacuated from the earth, the force that has been restraining evil will be removed, and the Antichrist will be revealed and step on to the world's stage.

The Holy Spirit wants us to be aware of and understand these world-changing events that are rapidly approaching. He is not trying to scare us, but to prepare us and ignite a passion in us to reach our unsaved family members, friends, and coworkers with the truth. He also wants us to guard ourselves from being contaminated by the mutinous, rebellious attitude that is quickly spreading in society.

The emphasis of this lesson:

Just because the world and a portion of the Church are falling into apostasy, it doesn't mean we have to do the same. If we'll listen to and obey God's Word, we can float on the waters of adversity and rise above the destruction flooding our world — just as Noah did.

The Holy Spirit Emphatically Wants Us To Know Something About the Last of the Last Days

Under the inspiration of the Holy Spirit, the apostle Paul wrote, "Now the Spirit speaketh expressly, that in the latter times some shall depart from the faith, giving heed to seducing spirits, and doctrines of devils" (1 Timothy 4:1). Here we see Paul prophetically pointing His finger 2,000 years into the future to tell us what would take place at the end of the age.

First, notice the word "expressly." It is the Greek word *rhetos*, and it means *unmistakably* or *vividly*. It *pictures something spoken clearly or something that is unquestionable, certain, and sure.* By using the word *rhetos*, the Holy Spirit is telling us categorically and emphatically about something that is coming. It's almost as if He is reaching through the pages of Scripture to grab us and say, "Do you hear what I'm saying? I'm speaking in the strongest and clearest language because I want to make sure you understand what I'm saying because it will most certainly come to pass."

The period He notes for these events are the "latter times." The word "latter" is the Greek word *husteros*, which means *latter* and *pictures the ultimate end or the very last of something.* And the word "times" is the Greek word *kairos*, which describes *a season.* Together, *husteros kairos* — translated here as "latter times" — describes *the very last season or period of the Church age.* By using these words, the Holy Spirit gave us one of the major signs that we are living in the very end of the age.

'Some Shall Depart from the Faith'

What can we know without question will happen when there is no more time remaining? Paul said, "…Some shall depart from the faith…" (1 Timothy 4:1). The word "depart" in this verse is vital. It is the Greek word *aphistemi*, which is a compound of the words *apo*, meaning *away*, and the word *histimi*, meaning *to stand*. When these words are compounded, they form the word *aphistemi*, which means *to stand apart from; to distance one's self from; to step away from; to withdraw from; or to shrink away from*. It is from this very Greek word that we derive the word *apostate* or *apostasy*.

As unbelievable as it may seem, the Holy Spirit is telling us that at the very end of the Church Age, when no time remains, "…some shall *depart* from the faith…." This is not an abrupt rejection of the faith. It is *a very gradual withdrawal* that takes place steadily over a period of time. It is the picture a person who slowly but surely changes the position of what he or she once believed. Instead of holding firmly to the faith, they begin to entertain other options and ideas that progressively lead them away from what they once believed. This departure is so gradual that those who are in the process of withdrawing may not even realize it is happening.

Thankfully not everyone will depart from the faith. The Bible says only "some," which in Greek signifies *a very notable some*. This suggests that a number of these people may be individuals we once looked to, listened to, and trusted. But for some reason, they will shrink away from the pure truth they once believed and taught.

Specifically, they will depart from "the faith." In Greek, this is the word *pisteos*, and it refers to *doctrine* or *to the long-held, time-tested teachings of Scripture*. What is interesting here is that it includes a definite article. In other words, this is not talking about a departure from faith in miracles or faith in healing per se. It is a slow drifting from "THE faith" — *the clear, timeless teaching of Scripture*.

'Giving Heed to Seducing Spirits'

This raises the question: Why will some depart from the faith? The Bible says it will result from them "…giving heed to seducing spirits and doctrines of devils" (1 Timothy 4:1). The phrase "giving heed" is the Greek word *prosecho*. It is the compound of the word *pros*, which means *to lean toward*, and the word *echo*, which means *to hold* or *to embrace*. When the words *pros* and *echo* are joined to form the word *prosecho*, it pictures *a person who has believed one thing for a very long time but is now leaning in a new direction, believing something else.* They have opened their mind to possibilities other than Scripture, and slowly-but-surely, they have withdrawn from what they once held precious and dear and have begun to hold on to new ideas and new systems of belief.

Eventually, those who depart from the faith and fail to repent and turn back to God, end up totally rejecting the faith. We see this happening in the world today. Well-known Christian authors and ministers who were once stalwarts of truth have recanted what they stood by and taught for decades. Some have even begun to modify what they believe is right and wrong about gender. As the world around us rapidly changes, many don't know how to fit into it. Consequently, rather than standing on biblical truth that is absolute and unchanging, they begin to entertain the idea of modifying the faith to fit into the new emerging world. And the end result is disastrous apostasy.

What is influencing these individuals to change their position and leave the clear teaching of Scripture? Through Paul, the Holy Spirit identified "seducing spirits and doctrines of demons" as the culprit. The word "seducing" is a translation of the Greek word *planao*, which means *to wander*. It pictures *deception, moral wandering, or deviant behavior.* Moreover, it depicts *a person (or nation) that has veered from a solid path, and as a result of veering morally, this person (or nation) is adrift.*

At the time of the New Testament, the majority of the world spoke Greek. It was the international language used even by rabbis — especially the Jewish rabbis who lived in Alexandria that did a great deal of writing. They were very familiar with the word *planao* and understood its meaning.

Interestingly, the word *planao* was also used to depict *a lost animal that had veered so far from the path that it couldn't find its way back home.* The use of this word tells us the activity of seducing spirits causes people to leave the well-established path of God's Word that they — and countless others — have walked on for a long time. In fact, the implication here is that they have walked on this well-worn path so long they could probably walk it blindfolded. But when seducing spirits begin to operate, they deceive people into leaving the path and veering into new territory. The ultimate goal of seducing spirits is to push people off a spiritual cliff and destroy them.

Doctrines of Demons

There is another force at work in these last of the last days, and the Bible identifies it as "doctrines of devils." The word "doctrines" in First Timothy 4:1 is the Greek word *didaskalia*, which describes *a well-packaged teaching that is applicable to a lifestyle*. Thus, when it is presented, the error will sound logical and appeal to one's flesh. People will hear it and say, "Wow! That's a possibility I should consider." In other words, when the devil comes knocking on your door, he doesn't show up with horns on his head, a protruding tail, and a red pitchfork in his hand. On the contrary, he comes with the slickest PR infomercial ever produced. He offers ideas that are tantalizing and mesmerizing in an effort to get you to accept his invitation and veer from the path of Scripture.

Make no mistake. Behind these well-packaged systems of thought that are being promoted are "devils." The word "devils" is the Greek word *daimonion*, which in context, describes *evil spirits, demons, devils*. The ancient world believed demons thickly populated the lower regions of the air and that spirits were the primary cause of disasters, suffering, and actions of insanity. At the time of the New Testament, if someone was insane, thinking crazy, or acting like a lunatic, it was believed that person had a demon.

Just stop and think about some of the people in society today who are promoting their bold, new progressive policies. You've seen them in the headlines and heard their multiple soundbites, spouting and touting their outlandish philosophies. Taken at face-value, their ideas are sheer lunacy. These bizarre leaders claim to have the answers to everything we're facing, when in fact they are campaigning for chaos and catastrophe. What's behind all this nonsense? The Bible says its "seducing spirits and doctrines of devils."

Again, the Holy Spirit makes this clear through the apostle Paul in First Timothy 4:1: "Now the Spirit speaketh expressly, that in the latter times some shall depart from the faith, giving heed to seducing spirits, and doctrines of devils." In the very strongest and clearest of terms that cannot be misunderstood, the Holy Spirit urgently warned us that when we've come to the very end of the Church age and no time remains, some people — even those who are notable — shall begin to slowly but surely put distance between themselves and the clear, sound teaching of Scripture.

This will be the work of seducing spirits and doctrines of demons who bring well-packaged alternative ideas and lifestyles to lead people astray.

Friend, stick with the truth. Make the decision to press into the timeless, unchanging truth of God's Word every day and get to know the Holy Spirit of God who authored it. These two practices will go a long way to help keep your head on straight in a world gone crazy!

STUDY QUESTIONS

> Study to shew thyself approved unto God, a workman that needeth not to be ashamed, rightly dividing the word of truth.
> — 2 Timothy 2:15

1. What does God say in His Word about sticking to His tried and true path of old? Check out these passages of Scripture and identify what He promises to those who don't veer off track. (*See* Jeremiah 6:16; Psalm 16:11; 119:35; Proverbs 4:18.)
2. The Bible says, "See to it that no one carries you off as spoil or makes you yourselves captive by his so-called philosophy and intellectualism and vain deceit (idle fancies and plain nonsense)…" (Colossians 2:8 *AMPC*). How can you guard yourself from swallowing deception and departing from the faith? Consider Colossians 2:6,7; Romans 12:2; and Second Timothy 3:14-17.

PRACTICAL APPLICATION

> But be ye doers of the word, and not hearers only, deceiving your own selves.
> — James 1:22

1. The Holy Spirit emphatically stated that in latter times some would depart from the faith. Who do you know that once held tightly to Scripture but has gradually walked away from truth and is now embracing practices that are totally against God's Word? Can you see how and where they began drifting away from the truth? What can you learn from their example to protect yourself from experiencing the same outcome?
2. Hebrews 2:1 (*MSG*) says, "It's crucial that we keep a firm grip on what we've heard so that we don't drift off." This "drifting off" is

departing from the faith — *it's distancing one's self from, stepping away from, and slowly withdrawing from the timeless truth of Scripture.* Take a moment to pray and ask God these vital questions and listen for His answers.

- *"Father, have I drifted into this subtle, almost imperceptible pattern of departure? Am I unknowingly being influenced by seducing spirits and doctrines of demons?"*

- *"If I have, where am I adrift? In what ways have my beliefs deviated from the truth?"*

- *"Father, please forgive me. Show me what I can do to stay anchored in the truth of Your Word. In Jesus' name, Amen."*

Notes